Hippocrates, RN

To
Pat Ruffell Smith

Hippocrates, RN

Memoirs of a Naval Flying Doctor

HERBERT ELLIS, AFC

ROBERT HALE · LONDON

Frist published in Great Britain 1988
Reprinted 1988

ISBN 0 7090 3269 2

Robert Hale Limited
Clerkenwell House
Clerkenwell Green
London EC1R 0HT

British Library Cataloguing in Publication Data

Ellis, W.H.B.
Hippocrates, RN: memoirs of a naval flying doctor
1. Great Britain. Medicine. Ellis, W.H.B.
I. Title
610′.92′4

ISBN 0-7090-3269-2

The author would like to point out that the ranks attributed to people in the book are appropriate to events at the time. Many of course, were to change later.

Photoset in North Wales by
Derek Doyle & Associates, Mold, Clwyd.
Printed in Great Britain by
St Edmundsbury Press Ltd, Bury St Edmunds, Suffolk.
Bound by WBC Bookbinders Limited.

Contents

We have fed our sea for a thousand years
And she calls us, still unfed.

Rudyard Kipling

Hippocrates knew little of anatomy or physiology, and he had neither clinical thermometer nor stethoscope. It is true that he employed auscultation, placing his ear to the chest of the patient and describing, for example, the friction sound of pleurisy, which he aptly likened to the creaking of leather. But although he had no scientific apparatus, he had scientific method, and his writings are full of sound observation and logical reasoning.

He advises the physician about to set up practice in an unfamiliar town, to observe the exposure, the prevailing winds, the water supply, the nature of the soil and the habits of the people. From this information, he will be able to deduce what diseases are the most prevalent, and will thus achieve the greatest triumphs in the practice of his art.

Douglas Guthrie, *A History of Medicine*.

List of Illustrations

Diagrams

Picture Credits

Author: 1, 2, 4, 6, 20, 21, 23; RAF Museum, Hendon: 3; Ann Ruffell Smith: 5, 7; Rear-Admiral I.G.W. Robertson: 8, 25; Commander R.H. Reynolds: 9-11, 13-18; D.H. James: 12; J. Waterman: 19, 24; Harold Salisbury: 22

Acknowledgements

Some Mandatory, Some Whimsical

The author wishes to pay tribute to the following:

The Admiralty and especially those Fleet Air Arm Officers in the 1940s and 1950s tolerant enough to accept a medical officer into their exclusive club.

The Royal Air Force Institute of Aviation Medicine, Farnborough, for providing a haven for many years, and especially to IAM's present commandant, Air Vice Marshal Peter Howard OBE, for his help in searching out photographs and for his assistance in rekindling some of the memories recounted.

The United States Navy, Bureau of Medicine and Surgery, and my many American friends, both military and civilian, who made me feel so welcome in their workspaces and in their homes.

My children, Penelope and Christopher, for reading the manuscript, their amused tolerance at my endless prattling. ('It's all right till you try and be funny, Dad.')

My step-daughter Joanna and her tireless efforts to teach me grammar, correcting the manuscript when she came down from her eyrie at Oxford, where she had the advantage (an unfair one, I thought) of reading English.

The countless Air Traffic Control officers who entered into the spirit as well as the world, so enthusiastically, of the airborne 'surgery', interpreting some of the medical terms transmitted over the ether.

My patient, long-suffering neighbour Ann Courtenay Lord for deciphering my medical scrawl and transposing it into typescript.

The Times for permission to reproduce the obituary notice of Group Captain H.P. Ruffell Smith.

Annette Ruffell Smith for her help in making documents available and her part in the compilation of some of the facts.

The editor of *Wingspan*, Derek James for the loan of the photograph of the Meteor deck landing.

The Royal Air Force Museum for permission to reproduce some of the photographs, and the Fleet Air Arm Officers' Association for similar help, in particular Commander R.H. Reynolds, DSC, AFC.

Harold Salisbury, who, when not acting as a Chief Constable, has risked his life and camera in the air and on the road and finally cornered me in a museum, perhaps fittingly, in one of the pictures.

Michael Fopp, Director of the RAF Museum Hendon, and his staff for their kind and patient help with illustrations.

The countless friends who have given encouragement at moments when I have felt inclined to stop, not believing that such tales could hold any interest for a modern reader.

Particularly to The Hon. Sir John Thompson for suggesting the title – no doubt inspired by our proximity at the time to the Greek island of Kos.

Finally and most important, my thanks to my long-time friend and mentor Rear-Admiral Ian Robertson CB, DSC, who chanced his life and professional career in the early days by 'pushing me out of the nest'.

Foreword

Nowadays it is commonplace to watch on our television screens the almost regular trips of the American shuttle to and from outer space. Every day we know that thousands of miles are flown by the world's airlines, yet we barely give the matter a thought unless, unhappily, we are reminded of this fact by an accident or mishap. Our military aviators are exercising combat tactics in support of the maritime and land forces, in very sophisticated and highly complex aircraft, beyond or near the speed of sound, at great altitudes or at tree-top height, depending on the tactical situation prevailing. Deck landings are now considered simple, with the advent of angled decks, mirror sights and other electronic aids.

Because we are 'brainwashed' by the manufacturers, telling us of the technical brilliance of their designers, technicians and products, we tend to forget those members of aircrew who through this period of fantastic mechanical advance have had to cope with the physical and physiological changes which aviators of thirty and more years ago would have thought impossible. Witness, as a simple example, a fast jet pilot's personal flying-clothing: suits, helmets, breathing equipment, G-tolerance waistcoats and survival gear, all costing many thousands of pounds.

For all this we must acknowledge the work done by pioneers like Dr Herbert Ellis.

In 1946 Surgeon Lieutenant W.H.B. Ellis, Royal Navy, and I shared a cabin at the Royal Naval Air Station at Gosport, Hants. I was teaching young sub-lieutenants how to fly in Tiger Moths. I don't think that W.H.B.E. was overworked; in fact, I am sure he was rather bored, as we were all pretty fit in those days! Naturally he wanted to have a ride to gain some air experience, since he was living and dealing with aircrew and students in his surgery and wardroom mess.

I see from my logbook that it was on 20 November 1946 that I took him up in Tiger Moth G for George. After the usual patter I gave him the controls and in an instant realized that here was a 'natural'. After only four hours and fifty minutes dual instruction, on April Fools Day 1947 I stepped out of the aeroplane, secured the straps and told him to go solo, and do one circuit and landing. Looking back, I suppose we broke every rule in the book, but who cared? W.H.B.E. did a perfect landing and, as events have proved, a dedicated aviator came into being.

Events forced Dr Ellis to retire from the Royal Navy but, as can be seen in *Hippocrates RN*, not until he had made his mark and had contributed greatly to aviation medicine. He has since been very successful in the commercial field. He still practises medicine but, after forty years of treasured friendship, I know that his heart is still in flying, particularly naval aviation.

The Royal Navy and the British Aerospace Industry have every reason to be grateful for Dr Ellis's research and pioneering efforts which have so notably assisted in the development of all aspects of human behaviour of those who are of the flying profession.

Rear-Admiral I.G.W. Robertson CB, DSC.

Introduction: *Farnborough*

I was sceptical when I was 'instructed' to write a diary about my days at Farnborough for, although these days could be numbered amongst the happiest and in many ways most rewarding of my life, it was not immediately apparent that they would be of the slightest interest to people not connected with flying at that time.

My literary agent begged to differ, but the reasons he put forward for so doing had a certain sting in the tail. 'Do you realize,' he said, 'that this is part of history?' Not for the first time had it been impressed upon me that I was not just *getting* but actually *was* old! To be realistic, in the flying world we become 'old' at a refreshingly young age, for in aviation machines and techniques become out of date very quickly, as new discoveries and inventions are made, and a pilot can easily find that technological developments have outrun his mastery of them.

One day, not many years ago, driving on my daily medical rounds near Bath, I found myself following the road around the RAF base at Colerne. I saw a number of aircraft parked on the airfield and realized they were very familiar: a Meteor, a Canberra, a Viking and many others. I felt young again, for I had flown most of the aircraft I was looking at – the sight of them wove a spell over my imagination and I recalled their handling characteristics, approach speeds, vices and virtues. I could smell the burning kerosene, hear the musical whine of the jets. I felt young again; I felt exhilarated. I was then brought down to earth with a jolt as I saw a notice which solemnly informed me that I was approaching the RAF Museum of Historical Aircraft.

My agent was right: history *is* important and should be recorded before it is lost for ever. I have therefore attempted to recall some of the happy, often hilarious moments of a carefree period in the development of British aviation with an emphasis on human performance and behaviour, in which I was both privileged and fortunate enough to play a small part. As in all research, much time and effort appear to be unfruitful and even wasted, but I have learnt that no time spent in serious activity is truly lost.

If undue emphasis appears to have been placed on mistakes and jollity in this story, I would remind the reader that one does not read about ordinary events, only the exceptions: the train that runs late, the ship that sinks, the aircraft that doesn't arrive. For all the episodes that I have chosen to relate to you that might seem foolhardy or careless, there were hundreds of routine, experimental and often dull episodes that would seem boring if recounted in detail, thousands of uneventful sorties flown by medical pilots in pursuit of facts, research etc.

I hope you will be able to share some of the joys and satisfaction that I was privileged to experience during the fruitful early post-war years of the Farnborough 'Lab'. The Empire Test Pilots School, also then situated at Farnborough, trained experienced pilots from all over the world. It was no coincidence that the standard of airmanship at Farnborough achieved a level which set a standard for the world. It enabled the main task of flying to be discharged with minimum encumbrance from regulations, red tape etc. It is an era which is unlikely to recur.

A decision had to be taken as to whether these jottings should be recorded in a manner which provided a physiological record of findings, and so risk the charge of attempting to write yet another textbook on aviation medicine, or whether to record a series of events in a light-hearted way and hope to interest a wider readership. In the event the choice was easy, for when I came to read my thesis on the matters in which I gained my doctorate of medicine, it was patently the dullest book imaginable.

The thesis was painstakingly put together from a series of scientific papers on the more serious aspects of the airborne experiments. Eventually, when completed, I sent it to my old medical school at Durham University in support of my doctorate. It clearly caused consternation amongst the worthy clinicians up there – more used to a thesis with titles such as 'Infestation by haystack mites in extra-marital coitus – a review of ninety-eight cases'. When I had not received acknowledgement of my thesis, I telephoned the Dean of Medicine's office, and an embarrassed secretary admitted that the Dean could not make up his mind whether the thesis should be read by the Medical Faculty or passed to the Aeronautical Society. However, they determined that I should be examined on my thesis by an external examiner, and I was to present myself at Cambridge on a certain date.

Shortly afterwards I was told to attend on Dr Roland Winfield, who was a most eminent doctor experienced on Spitfires and many other World War II aircraft. I believe he was more impressed by the Mosquito bomber in which I had ferried myself to Marshall's Field, Cambridge, than by the wretched thesis so carefully strapped to the navigator's seat. At all events, he signified approval, though the nature of the *viva voce* indicated that he viewed the meeting in the nature of one eccentric talking to another. At one point in the proceedings taking place in his study, the most delightfully untidy one I have ever seen, he enquired as to the suitability of the room temperature. As I was visibly blue with cold, he reached down beneath his desk and picked up two lengths of flex, which he wired together with Elastoplast. After he had thrown a switch big enough to stop Battersea Power Station, the bare wires glowed into life. I felt I was in the presence of a 'great' man.

1 *In the Beginning ...*

Lucky is the youngster who both knows what he wants to do with his life *and* manages to achieve that ambition. In my case I was destined to be the vehicle of my father's failed ambitions. He was an admirer of the medical profession and had suffered a fractured vertebra as the result of jumping out of his aircraft as it was shot down in World War I – an injury which, ironically, I repeated some twenty-five years later – and he was determined that I should fulfil his own unrealized hopes. He had enlisted in the Royal Flying Corps and probably owed his life to the fact that he was taken prisoner by the Germans at an early stage. After the war he was co-founder of the Newcastle-on-Tyne Aero Club, so I was exposed (literally in those days) to flying at a very early age while sitting on my mother's knee for my first 'air-experience' flights. I recall bitter disappointment at not being surrounded by flocks of birds!

I well remember happy days when my father and mother, armed with a wicker picnic basket, and me sitting on mother's knee (modern-day bureaucracy would soon have stopped that!), would fly up the Northumbrian coast and land on a deserted beach. When we were ready to return, Mother would sit in the cockpit and Father would shout 'Contact!' before swinging the propeller, jumping in and flying back to Cramlington. It all seemed a magic world to a three-year-old boy, and the memory probably started the train of events which made this book possible.

I had a further, but unfortunate, taste of flying whilst at school at Oundle. As a conscript in the school OTC, my company commander was Arthur Marshall, the broadcaster, who would come on parade with an umbrella. He told me my marching was appalling, and my feet, like my French verbs, were never in the right place, so I had better join the air section. Unwittingly he did me a good turn, though I was sorry to miss his antics on formal parades.

The air section was taken for air experience to RAF Wittering. On one such visit we were taken up in Blenheims. After take-off we were soon in cloud and, whilst my pilot concentrated on his instruments, I nervously peered outside at the 'fog', for I knew we had followed another Blenheim into the cloud, and this aircraft had another boy, Denis Nahum, as a passenger. Almost imperceptibly at first, I made out the gloomy shape of the other aircraft and its tail just above our starboard propeller, but getting rapidly closer. I tapped my pilot on the shoulder and in looking up he pulled the control column slightly back, sufficient to get our propeller into the tail of the other aircraft. I remember every detail of the next few minutes, even though nearly fifty years have passed. The tail of the other aircraft was sliced clean through and disappeared, swept away in the slipstream. I next heard a klaxon horn (the undercarriage warning) as my pilot closed his throttles and went into a steep dive, soon emerging from cloud. I could see the green grass of RAF Wittering below, and our starboard propeller stopped, the blades twisted. I momentarily saw an open parachute beneath us and a developing plume of smoke rising from the ground before we landed with one engine out of action.

The whole episode had probably lasted no more than three minutes but an incident of untold heroism had been enacted and a man had given his life to save that of another.

Until the aircraft collided, there was no warning of the imminent danger. Denis was sitting behind his pilot with his chest-type parachute unclipped beside him – in accordance with practice. His pilot, Sergeant Pilot Bull, on losing his controls, turned his attention towards saving his schoolboy passenger. In spite of the aircraft gyrating out of control, according to Dennis, Bull clipped Dennis' parachute to his chest by one clip only and physically pushed him out of the aircraft, pulling his ripcord as he left. Sergeant Pilot Bull had no time to leave and perished in the wreckage.

Soon my developing fascination for aeroplanes had to be temporarily laid aside, for my father had other plans for me.

When I was about fourteen years old, my father, having cursorily enquired as to my intention in life, proceeded to formulate my career for me in line with his own failed ambition. 'This country is going to the Left,' he said, 'and most things will be nationalized. The one thing that can't be touched is medicine, as it involves people – so I've arranged for you, as an introduction, to watch an operation which will be performed by my friend Mr J. Hamilton Barclay tomorrow morning. Please be at the hospital prompt at 9.45.'

I knew nothing of medicine, fainted in sympathy if anyone else fainted and felt queasy if I cut my own finger, but I knew there was little option but to present myself at No. 2 Theatre on the next day as instructed.

The Royal Victoria Infirmary, Newcastle-on-Tyne, at which J. Hamilton Barclay MS, FRCS, was Professor of Surgery, was built in the imposing but grim Victorian style. It imbued a sense of foreboding to anyone crossing its portals for the first time, giving an impression of being capable of totally digesting anyone daring to enter, never to be seen again.

I found myself walking down interminable corridors, the air pungent with the odour of antiseptic, and apprehensively went through the doors marked 'No. 2 Theatre – Strictly No Admission' (in itself, I recall thinking, a denial of the objective). The wanderings down endless corridors on my way to the operating theatre had preconditioned my outlook to that of Alice through the Looking Glass. They reminded me of the London Tube system but without the trains and railway lines. The 'tube' would one moment be running level before dipping down a long incline, cutting off one's view, so that it seemed to have no end. The tunnels (for by this time I was indeed Alice in my mind) were inhabited by gowned troglodytes with surgical masks and white wellington boots, though the significance of the red stains on the boots escaped me at that time. Some troglodytes were pushing fellow trogs lying prone on trolleys, apparently having a sleep. It seemed to be an unreal but not unattractive world. I espied one notice on a door stating authoritatively, 'This door must be kept locked shut.' How curious, I mused – what use would be served if it was kept locked open?

I continued down the tunnel and passed another side door marked 'Pharmacy – we dispense with care.' Some years later I realized why I have always looked upon chemists with some suspicion.

I remember an overwhelming stench of ether, coupled with an aroma of what I can only recall as 'warm wind' and, as I was ushered, by this time gowned, through the final door to the amphitheatre itself, I was confronted with a scene reminiscent of a Klu Klux Klan meeting and a pair of eyes belonging to the Professor. His gloved right hand was holding a gleaming scalpel, poised as I entered, above a heaving piece of bared white skin. The last I remember was a widening 'smile' as the scalpel parted the abdominal skin into what seemed like bleeding cherry-red lips. Then blessed oblivion, till I came round in the recovery room, to which I had beaten the patient by a short head.

Notwithstanding this, I did qualify and in 1944 became

the Professor's house surgeon, taking my turn in removing appendices in that same operating theatre several years later.

One further incident should be recorded. During my student days I chanced to meet Sir William Beveridge and accompanied him on his electioneering campaigns, as a prospective Liberal candidate, around Northumberland. I was spellbound as he recounted his plans for what amounted to the nationalization of medical practice, later published as the Beveridge Plan. He became Lord Beveridge, and his 'plan' turned into the National Health Service.

During medical training, I applied to join the Royal Navy. For as long as I could remember I had set my heart on becoming a naval officer, influenced by boyhood holidays spent at Bamburgh on the north-east coast. When I submitted my application to the Admiralty, I was relieved to be told that I would be considered as soon as I had passed my final examinations, so I directed all my efforts to that end.

Perhaps I should mention at this point that my choice of career in the Navy was influenced by one other factor: I was – and still am – terrified of women. If I was to practise medicine, what better place to do so than in the Navy, where even to mention a woman's name on certain occasions was to lay oneself open to stand a round of drinks.

But before I reached that haven, I must still confront women patients …

While I was a clinical student, gaining experience in administering light anaesthetics, on one occasion my patient was an attractive young woman who required a minor operation on her leg. My task was to administer a mixture of nitrous oxide and oxygen – I was about to discover why it is called 'laughing gas'. This anaesthetic had the twin virtues of being easy to administer and being followed by a rapid recovery. However, during the recovery phase, it makes the patient, pass through a brief period of mental confusion, characterized by euphoria and fantasy, often of an amorous nature.

I was standing at the head of the operating table holding the patient's head and jaw, to ensure she had a satisfactory airway, when she opened her eyes, gazed at my face for a few seconds and then exclaimed: 'Oh, can I have you for Christmas?' Gales of laughter came from the operating staff to the complete embarrassment of myself and the patient, who by this time had re-emerged into the real world. I learned the lesson from this episode never to examine a female patient without a third party being present.

I well recall one particular lesson in objectivity. As students we were taught to approach cases in just this way, without emotional involvement. We were also taught to observe and report facts, not impressions. A keen advocate of such a principle was Dr Bernard Shaw, Professor of Pathology and a nephew of the great George Bernard Shaw. He was a brusque, stern man, whose forbidding appearance concealed a shy and kind personality.

Shaw would hold seminars for his pathology students specifically designed to sharpen their powers of observation, during which non-medical questions would be posed. An apocryphal story concerns the role the pathology department played in urinalysis. He would produce a specimen glass of urine and explain that such a specimen should be examined 'like wine'. First, hold it up to the light – for translucency, as a cloudy specimen might indicate a feverish patient or an old specimen; secondly it should be examined for odour, for this could reveal decaying pus cells indicating possible renal disease. 'And now,' he would explain, 'you must literally taste it – possibly to detect a sweetness, indicating diabetes.' He hastened to concede that this last act could be repugnant so, like wine, tasting only a small quantity would suffice –

he demonstrated by dipping a finger into the liquid and sipping it. He would then seek confirmation from his class that the lesson had been truly learned and also that all the students were willing to carry out this somewhat unusual investigation before passing the specimen jar round the class, watching the while as the class followed his instructions. Having completed the exercise, he would then pour the remains of the urine down the sink and, with the ghost of a smile discernible on his usually stern, expressionless face, fix his class over the top of his spectacles.

'I am encouraged to note that, without exception, you have proved to my satisfaction that you have shown yourselves prepared to do unpleasant, even repugnant things. I would ask you, however, to sharpen your powers of observation if you are not to miss some vital sign in a possibly fatal disease. If you had observed my action more diligently, you would have seen that, when it came to tasting the specimen, whereas I dipped my forefinger into the glass, I actually tasted my middle finger!'

Having studied pharmacology, the mysteries of dispensing were imparted to us by the head pharmacist, Mr Foggin, in a series of brief, practical, down-to-earth talks. Here is a world, one can certainly argue today, with as much influence over man's destiny as that of nuclear physics. To be able to influence, even control, human desires, temperament and character by the administration of a chemical (without the recipient necessarily being aware) was power indeed. Mr Foggin went to considerable lengths to stress the importance of not breaking faith with our patients and the trust which they placed in our prescribing. He drilled his class in the manner of a sergeant major drilling officer cadets at Sandhurst, admonishing in a kindly manner but with the knowledge that his young squad would shortly be despatched into the world with a 'licence to kill', as he put it.

He suffered frequent attacks of angina pectoris.

Whenever he felt his protégés were giving less than the required level of attention, he would pause and give a masterful imitation of an anginal attack (or was it? – he died of a coronary thrombosis some few years later). He would screw his face up and fumble for a tablet, which he would place under his tongue, with near immediate beneficial results.

'That's what TNT can do for you,' he would say, sure in the knowledge that he now had one hundred per cent attention. 'Remember it is the *art* of medicine you've got to master – it is not a science. Your patients will come to see you, often at considerable trouble to themselves and frequently for nothing more than reassurance, and you have something of the standing of a priest in their eyes. Return the compliment. Feel the pulse, remember the biblical value of the laying-on of hands. Ensure that they feel they have the benefit of your undivided and unhurried attention. Remember to treat the person as well as the disease.'

He would continue on his own particular theme: 'Above all, give them a bottle of something, anything; they will expect it. Add some colouring matter if it makes it look more appealing!' After an impressive pause, possibly broken by a further sub-lingual TNT tablet, he would then add, 'Make your patient go away and come back for the medicine – they will value it the more, regarding it as specially made up for them. In this way you will have created the twin ingredients of *desire* and *faith* – so essential for medicines and the power of healing to work together.'

At this point he would again pause impressively before moving to what he clearly believed to be the climax of his advice.

'Most important of all, however, is presentation. Whatever you elect to put into the bottle, wrap it up in clean, crisp white paper with the ends neatly tucked in and sealed with sealing wax – different colours for different medicines, thus reinforcing the impression of individuality for the patient.' As it was war-time, this was quite a concession to the rigours of paper shortage.

I well recall listening to this address with rapt attention, for I had recently read *Dr Bradley Remembers,* a novel by Francis Brett Young about a doctor and seen Robert Donat in *The Citadel* – both of which reinforced the idyllic impression of Victorian medicine at its best and as portrayed by Mr Foggin. That he was right I don't dispute, for many of his ideas have since been taken up by commercial firms whether they package foods, clothes or even DIY goods. By contrast, medicines now come in tablet form in small bottles and the pharmacological power contained therein is as relevant to the liquids dispensed in my student days as a nuclear warhead is to an airgun.

Thus equipped with an ability to 'package' and armed with a slim booklet entitled *The British Pharmocopoeia,* I was launched upon my healing career.

The results of the final examinations were pinned up, and the struggling mass of would-be doctors sorted themselves out into the successful ones and those who would have to return to their studies. Having passed, I applied for a locum tenens appointment in a small, single-handed practice at Stocksfield, a country village up the Tyne Valley, to gain experience whilst awaiting instructions from the Admiralty. The people of Stocksfield, like most Northumbrian country folk, were reticent and retiring, slow to accept strangers into their midst. They were hardy, going about their daily tasks breathing some of the purest air to be found in England – fresh from the Cheviots, scented by the pine forests and with the sound of rushing water carried on the wind coming down the Tyne Valley, the sort of setting beloved by script-writers of medical stories. And so it was that I walked onto the set in all my innocence.

I arrived, somewhat apprehensively, at the second

largest house in the village – the largest belonged to the vicar. It was an old-fashioned square Georgian house with a newly polished brass plate on the gate pillar. I was met in the driveway by an agitated man looking at his watch, rather like the White Rabbit. 'Come on, young fellow, I've got to be off or I'll miss the boat train.' I felt uneasy for the first time since qualifying, for I had expected to have a little while to learn something about the practice, any seriously ill patients, maternity cases (God forbid, I thought), knowledge of the local chemist and a hundred other things.

'What about treatment?' I asked.

'Treatment?' asked the incumbent. 'Oh, that's simple. I'll show you.'

Leading me through his surgery, where the most conspicuous pieces of furniture were an old-fashioned roll-top desk and a horse-hair couch with some ominous stains on it, he said, 'I've found these urns to be the most effective way of getting people back on their feet and returned to normality.' We were standing in a rather dingy back room beyond his surgery, lit by an oil lamp. I recalled *The Citadel*. He indicated four urns, each holding about one gallon of liquid, numbered 1, 2, 3 and 4 and fitted with a tap like that on a sherry cask – perhaps not altogether inappropriate, I mused. I took this back room to be the dispensary, as the shelves were lined with bottles of all shapes and sizes, their labels largely obscured by dust.

The doctor saw my gaze wandering and broke in on my thoughts. 'See these urns? They're numbered one to four. No. 1 is for diarrhoea; No. 2 is for constipation; No. 3 is for cough, and No. 4 is for fevers. Recommend a tot of brandy for the teetotallers – it works wonders. Just make sure you don't miss any acute illness – always prod their tummies if in doubt, and look down their throats for diphtheria, and you won't go far wrong. These four remedies will take care of ninety per cent of the first visits, and the rest can be discussed with the chemist – we work closely together and he'll stand by you till I come back.'

With a 'Come along, my dear. We must be off', he and his wife disappeared through the front door to the waiting taxi, and I was left alone except for the housekeeper, a kindly soul who clearly played a significant part in the health of the local community. 'You'll have time for a cup of tea before your first surgery at five o'clock,' she stated, and I was glad for a moment to size up my task.

Promptly at 5 p.m. I went through the waiting room to the surgery, wondering what sort of emergency awaited me, for in my recent hospital appointment *every* case was either urgent or an emergency. I felt rather like a conductor mounting the rostrum and was slightly disappointed to find only two people waiting: an old man, coughing, and a woman sitting rather uncomfortably, holding her abdomen. I declined to recall the recently departed incumbent's words regarding stomach-prodding. Sitting at the roll-top desk, I adjusted my stethoscope, my obligatory badge of office, although unsure in which party it was supposed to inspire confidence, and pressed the buzzer to summon the first case.

The old man entered, still coughing. 'I want some cough medicine, Doctor, please,' he said. I told him firmly that I would decide what he would have, endeavouring to preserve my professional dignity but feeling far from confident. I resisted a momentary temptation to give him a draught from No. 3 urn and bade him bare his chest to enable me to examine him. 'Come on – take your shirt right off, please!' As he reluctantly complied, I was recalling the advice of my professor of gynaecology: 'If you want to witness a bedroom farce, don't peer through the keyhole: open the door, otherwise you might miss something.' My patient looked at me quizzically for a moment before undoing his front buttons and allowing me to listen to his chest. He had clearly suffered from emphysema for many years. I instructed him to return at 8 p.m. for a bottle which he would find on the hall table. The old man started to speak, thought better of it and said, 'Very well, Doctor. Just as you say.' I thought I detected a half smile on his face as he disappeared.

I summoned the next case, the woman, who was still holding her abdomen. 'I haven't had a bowel movement for four days, Doctor.' I felt downhearted but again resisted the temptation to run off a sample from No. 2 urn and directed her also to return at eight o'clock for her treatment. The woman also attempted to speak but changed her mind.

Somehow, I thought, this does not seem to be working out quite as I had expected, but I persisted, holding on to my ideals of 'personalized' treatment. I dealt with the remaining few cases: a few sick notes and a young woman who wanted to be fitted with a 'coil'. I did not feel that this was my sort of medicine at this early stage in my career, and certainly I had no wish to see the population explosion helped by myself, albeit indirectly so I asked her to return in three weeks time – 'after your next period,' I said. 'But I haven't seen anything for seven weeks,' she said, so I made an appointment for her to attend the ante-natal clinic, realizing afterwards that I was just beginning to taste medicine as it really was in the outlying areas.

Once alone, I turned my attention to what I should put into the six-ounce medicine bottles in my efforts to raise the standard of medical treatment in this village. I'll give these good people something by which they can remember me, I thought. I recognized some familiar names and, with the aid of my *British Pharmocopoeia,* dispensed various medicines from the raw ingredients in the dusty dispensary bottles. (The word 'shelf life' was a term applied only to ageing spinsters in those days.) I then carefully wrapped them up in the approved way in white paper, which I had brought with me, and finally applied the sealing wax. Mr Foggin would have been proud of me, I reflected. Carefully writing the patient's name with directions as to dose on the label, I carried them to the hall table before going out to visit a house where there was what sounded like an acute appendix. I felt well satisfied with my work and thought of the relief which the individually dispensed medicines would bring to my newly found devotees. The acute appendix turned out to be a mild case of indigestion and had gone out to the pictures, so, after a call at the chemist to introduce myself, I returned home – to find devastation in the hall. The housekeeper was on her knees, mopping up liquid, and broken glass was strewn about. One of the medicine bottles had exploded evidently. The housekeeper did not show great concern.

'I hope you don't mind, Doctor,' she said. 'I saw what you had done. We had been meaning to throw those old medicines out for some time.'

My mind turned to the patients who were due to collect these bottles, but the housekeeper anticipated my thoughts and said, 'I didn't think you would mind, Doctor, but when the patients came back they asked if they might have their old medicines as, whilst they were sure you were very wise and up-to-date, they had got used to their old medicine and knew where they were. We just filled up their old bottles, which they had brought with them. Hope you won't take offence, Doctor.'

I was fast learning the usefulness of experience. Medicine, like other professions, has come a long way since those days, but I wonder if it is all progress?

2 *I Join the Navy*

After my six weeks as a locum in the winter of 1944-5 running the single-handed practice at Stocksfield on Tyne, I felt fully qualified to play the leading role in *The Citadel*. Nevertheless, it was with relief that I found myself entitled to wear naval uniform. However, more complications lay ahead.

By this time VJ-Day had come and gone. I waited at home increasingly restless and frustrated, but about six weeks passed before the postman delivered a letter which ordered me to 'repair' to my 'ship', which turned out to be the Royal Naval Barracks at Chatham. Enthusiasm re-kindled as I arrived at RNB where I formed part of a production line to carry out demobilization medical examinations on sailors only too eager to throw away their uniforms.

I seemed to be going the wrong way. The purpose of going to Chatham was to learn about the habits of the Navy. All I can remember learning was to drink pink gin standing up rather than beer sitting down. I also learned to avoid being caught in open spaces during the 'close' season, around 9 a.m. when the massed bands of the marines would march to the parade ground blasting away at 'Hearts of Oak' and return shortly afterwards playing 'Life on the Ocean Wave'. The interval between these two events was occupied by a ceremony called 'Colours', which involved playing the National Anthem. This was accompanied by a great deal of saluting and struggling to get the White Ensign to the top of a flagpole (not always successful at first attempt). I soon learned that it was socially safer to be examining an abdomen whilst these activities were in progress. Seasoned regulars informed me that, before venturing out of doors at this time, one had to know when, who, what and how to salute and face in the right direction – 'Bit like facing Mecca, old boy.'

I was relieved when I received a piece of paper announcing I was to repair (once again) aboard HMS *Angelo* – 'Additional for Disposal' – and to report to SS *Orion* at Liverpool. I did not like the terminology 'additional'. Did this mean superfluous? And did 'for disposal' mean being taken out to sea and thrown overboard?

SS *Orion* had been a luxury liner on the run to the Far East before being converted to a troopship. Stabilizers were things of the future, and we sailed from the Mersey in the teeth of a Force 9 gale adopting a twenty-two-degree rolling motion which was to persist for the next eight days.

I found myself in a small 'single' cabin with two bunks, one atop the other. I elected for the bottom one, reasoning that it would be less painful to fall out. I had reckoned without my cabinmate's stomach, yet another reason for always conducting a thorough examination before making a decision. My cabinmate, whose name was Wilfred, before leaving his home at Giggleswick, had been firmly instructed by his mother to eat '… everything that's placed before you – it will help your sea-sickness'. If nothing else, Wilfred was a devoted son, and he dutifully did as he was told, before rushing back to his bunk immediately above mine. It was not long before an amalgam of the previous meal came cascading down past my face, the greasy parts congealing out on the wooden supports like a candle spilling its wax. Wilfred meant well and had placed a bowl on the deck but little of his gastric effluent reached it. After

The author in a Gypsy Moth, circa 1924

The author's father,
W. Baxter Ellis at
Hendon in 1915 by his
Caudron-type machine

Lieutenant W. Baxter Ellis in 1915, aged 20: Pilot's licence No. 1804

The author aged 35

a couple of nights of cringing in my bunk behind this waterfall, I prescribed non-greasy fluids, and the downpour first eased and then ceased. However, this was then replaced by a gurgling reminiscent of James Watt's reciprocating steam engine labouring with an inadequate head of steam.

In due course we arrived in Malta 'for disposal' and I occupied myself doing various medical duties before being shipped to Naples in a veteran tank-landing craft. In Naples I found myself attached to the staff of Admiral Sir John Cunningham, Commander-in-Chief Mediterranean. The old boy had wisely taken a leaf out of Nelson's book and ensconced himself in the Villa Emma, and his choice of abode was warmly endorsed by the Neapolitans, who were by that time sick of the war and welcomed the return of the British.

The Admiral's flag lieutenant was Lieutenant-Commander Gerald Pawle, a squash player of international repute and later to become defence correspondent of *The Sunday Times*. His Churchill-like personality was surpassed only by that of his admiral, and he kept us all very much in order. A kindly man.

The senior medical officer on the Admiral's staff was Surgeon Lieutenant Dick Glover. Dick was 'senior' only in years; he was in his thirties and explained that it had been a difficult task to find a medical officer who was even more junior than himself to be his assistant. (I was learning fast that an 'assistant' was necessary to do the work.) Dick was a jolly, friendly man, easy to get on with, and the next three months passed in a haze of official functions interspersed with watching the Grand Opera House being brought back to life.

Professionally a good deal of time was devoted to public health matters. Typhoid had only recently been brought under control; gonorrhea had not. Matters were not helped by the American habit of receiving preventative but inadequate 'shots' of penicillin before setting forth on amorous exercises, whilst our sailors fought the good fight with condoms issued from sick-bay.

I had my first experience of hydroballistic missile testing during this time. Sailors in the post-nuptial phase attending my clinic would blame their misfortunes on the low tensile strength of the latex of which their condoms were made. I also suspected that the condoms issued from my sick-bay had exceeded their shelf life before being put to use. Storage instructions, 'Store in a cool, dark place', had not always been followed, and the previous summer had been particularly hot. (Adding to my suspicions, I noticed on some of the boxes that some wag had replaced the word 'store' with 'use'.) My sick-berth attendant and I devised a simple test to detect 'rubber fatigue'.

At that time my sick-bay was located on the top of the Castel dell' Ovo, a medieval island fortress clearly visible on the sea front about a mile to the west of Naples harbour. It was approached via a causeway along which visiting pedestrians would pass beneath the vertical wall of the fortress, on top of which the sick-bay was located. There was a vertical drop of about 130 feet from the sick-bay to the causeway below.

Our simple form of 'quality control' consisted of taking a condom from each batch of twelve, attaching it to a tap and inflating it with two quarts of water, which we estimated was well beyond even the British sailor's capacity. Disposal was effected by gingerly cradling the resultant quivering, jelly-like 'missile' and dropping it over the parapet. Many was the unsuspecting visitor who arrived drenched, having been caught in a sudden show of unheralded silent 'rain'.

With the run-down of the Services after the cessation of hostilities, I found myself back in Malta, first at the Naval Hospital Big'hi, where I was appointed, to my astonishment, as the anaesthetist. Professional pride forbids me from elaborating on some of the exciting happenings during this period. From there I moved to the

Fleet Air Arm Station at Hal Far, where I had my first taste, as a passenger, of shore-based naval flying.

My time as Station Medical Officer at Hal Far was eventful. Malta was a dumping-ground for unwanted aircraft, often straight from the factory production lines, from all over the Mediterranean theatre. Row upon row of Mitchell and Boston bombers lined the military roads between Hal Far and Luqa, now the island's airport. The Royal Navy was endeavouring to find a level where the post-war contraction would cease, a process which appears to have continued to this day. There was also an abundance of aircrew in varying degrees of frustration. Most were anxious to return to civilian life; a few wanted to transfer to regular commissions.

The mood following cessation of hostilities still pervaded, and throughout there was an air of uncertainty. It was not surprising that the wardroom bar was heavily patronized, and aircraft crashes seemed uncomfortably frequent even to my untrained mind. I found myself taking an ever-increasing interest in the pilots and their life-style, an interest that appeared to be welcomed.

My first attempt at accident research was after a Beaufighter crashed on take-off one afternoon, killing the pilot. I found that the trim setting for the tail had been at fully back – the pilot was doomed before he left the ground. A glance at the wardroom wine accounts provided the probably explanation.

Thereafter I spent a lot of time flying as a passenger with the Mosquito Squadron, taking care first to study the life-style of my prospective pilot. I found myself welcomed, and the early seeds for the next fifteen years were sown.

After a year I was brought home and appointed to the naval air station at Gosport, where I found myself sharing a 'cabin' with a man who was to have, and indeed still has, a great influence on my life, Lieutenant (later Rear-Admiral) Ian Robertson.

Ian was a flying-instructor, and his duties included taking sub-lieutenants flying in Tiger Moths, with the object of making all future naval officers familiar with flying. Whenever there was a spare half hour, Ian would ring me in the sick-bay and I would hurry down to the flight to be given a short flying lesson. After a few of these quite unauthorized trips, Ian – to my utter astonishment, for I had not appreciated that he had been teaching me to fly – climbed out of the aircraft, ominously tied his seat harness up and shouted 'Off you go!' It was reminiscent of taking my first appendix out, but on that occasion at least help was immediately to hand. Thus a few minutes later I was airborne alone, enjoying that most personal and satisfying of experiences known to every pilot, although this time with an ominous overtone: it was quite unofficial and unauthorized. If anyone had heard about this episode or there had been a mishap, a court martial would have been convened aboard HMS *Victory*, at which Ian and I would have played more than just a walking-on part. The consequences might have resulted in my settling down in a country practice and Ian's not going on to command one of the Navy's last big conventional aircraft-carriers HMS *Eagle*.

By this time, enthused with Ian's tolerance and encouragement, I had really caught the flying 'bug'. By coincidence the Admiralty was becoming concerned at the high accident rate associated with deck landing. As pilots nearly always appeared to be responsible for the accidents, the Naval Medical Department's views were sought, and so it came about that applications were invited for two naval doctors to study the problems. I was fortunate enough to undertake a naval flying course. For the next eighteen months I was fully occupied officially learning to fly, culminating in deck-landing training in Fireflies, at that time the Navy's offering to anti-submarine warfare.

The only condition laid down by the Admiralty before

agreeing to my full flying course, apart from my meeting the required medical standards, was that I should take a permanent commission in the Royal Navy. (I was still RNVR – Royal Navy Volunteer Reserve – at the time.) This was not a difficult decision to make. The National Health Service was already developing uncomfortable teething problems. I found naval personnel, and aviators in particular, a congenial, able and tolerant group of people. Having agreed, I applied for my name to be transferred to the permanent Navy List; my request was granted. A momentous step had been taken that was to alter the whole course of my life.

I had one misgiving. I was not at all certain that I would measure up to the rigorous conditions laid down for the medical examination. On the other hand I was confident that I was not a medical risk either to myself or to others, despite the fact that I was twenty-seven at the time, thirty per cent older than most embryo aviators. In fact, the Navy agreed with me and I was in.

In due course I was allotted to No. 8 Flying Training Course. After pre-flight training at Donibristle, near Rosyth, happy weeks were spent in glorious summer weather at Yatesbury in Wiltshire, flying Tiger Moths. There was one other doctor on the course, Surgeon Lieutenant 'Fin' Lennan.

For the most part the six weeks at Yatesbury were uneventful. The flying school was run by the Bristol Aeroplane Company under contract for the Air Ministry. Most of the instructors were Royal Air Force, but the chief flying instructor was a civilian, and the whole atmosphere was relaxed and informal, the weather untypically English, with cloudless skies throughout. It was a happy time but the serious purpose behind our 'holiday' was brought home to us when failures on the course were identified and their flying careers terminated. Of the thirty-three embryo pilots commencing the course, eleven were failed in the early stages, five were to lose their lives for various reasons, and only three eventually qualified as fully operational pilots.

One hopeful was removed due to his inability to follow the correct procedure at forced landing in the event of sudden engine failure, not an uncommon occurrence in those days. For this purpose a satellite field was used just over the Wiltshire Downs, between the A4 and A361 roads. After a demonstration with an instructor, the pupil would be despatched solo. He would fly over the hill to practise his forced landing with strict instructions not actually to land but, at the moment before touch-down, to open up the engine and repeat the exercise after climbing to a suitable height. After an hour without our 'hero' returning to base, a search was mounted and a lone aircraft was seen in a small field, with the pilot dejectedly standing beside it. An experienced instructor with a spare pilot was immediately despatched to land there. After several abortive attempts he succeeded in landing in what was a very small field, stopping only by means of a skilfully controlled ground loop. He taxied back, stopped the engine and went over to the quite unrepentant pupil.

'How on earth did you manage to land in this small field?' he asked.

'Oh!' said the unsuspecting pupil, 'I didn't land in *this* field – I landed in that large field over there but couldn't stop, so I came right on through the hedge.'

He was on the first train back to London the next day.

After we had completed elementary flying training at Yatesbury, our course moved on to the Royal Air Force station at Kirton-in-Lindsey, Lincolnshire, where we were taught to fly Harvard aircraft. I remember Kirton for three reasons.

Firstly, the informal greeting by the Station Commander, a group captain who seemed to relish recounting, at the bar on the first night, how two members of the previous naval course had crashed at night and burned to death. He seemed to bear a particular dislike for the Navy, born, I suspect, of envy. I spent more time with the RAF than with the Navy during my service life and have always found great co-operation from the RAF pilots. Very occasionally, as in any community, the odd personality turns up with a chip on his shoulder. In this case the officer pulled rank to vent his spleen on the Navy, to his own discredit and that of his service.

Secondly, as a result of this 'welcome' by the commanding officer, our course approached night flying with more than a little apprehension. However, I was developing a taste for aerobatics, without sufficient daytime flying-time allocated to satisfy this predilection. The solution lay in taking to doing aerobatics at night, much helped by the lights from the blast furnaces at the steelworks of Scunthorpe. Unfortunately the Harvards' propeller made a particularly high-pitched 'whine' during unusual manoeuvres, a trait I heard being commented upon in the local pub. I therefore had to desist before the identity of the 'night intruder' was discovered.

The third aspect of Kirton which I have cause to remember was that I was shown up as being less than adequate in my 'military bearing'. Lieutenant Leo Dunne DSC was the senior pupil on our course and, although he was most sympathetic to me both as a person and as a doctor, he was responsible for presenting the naval course as a smart body of men able to match our hosts, the RAF, on, as well as off, parade. In my darker moments I would liken him to the senior officer in a prisoner-of-war camp.

I was shown up in my worst light on formal parades and 'square-bashing'. I still fail to see the connection between prowess on the parade ground and in the air – unless one sees the Red Arrows as an airborne equivalent of Trooping the Colour. After all, I reasoned, I was a doctor, and a bedside manner was the antithesis of arm-swinging and being shouted at in a loud voice across a parade ground, and indeed was the reverse to listening to a heart murmur down a stethoscope. So the morning parades loomed and

I, along with the others, would contrive to present some impression of unity as we marched down to the flights. Leo Dunne would attempt to hide me in the middle of his squad but this was becoming increasingly difficult. Not only did the red between my gold stripes stand out conspiciously as my arm swung out of time with the others, but the failure rate meant that, as time passed, there were fewer bodies in whose midst I might be camouflaged.

A problem loomed: how to cope with the forthcoming 'wings' parade, which would be attended by an admiral and full supporting dignitaries. Many plans were contrived, including my borrowing a uniform without the conspicuous red between the stripes. This was abandoned, for I would still stand out in the reviewing marchpast, and the executive Navy would be shown up in a bad light for allowing one of their number on parade who was clearly unable to exhibit even the first rudiments of parade-ground ceremony.

It was finally decided to revert to the original ploy of hiding me in the middle of the column when it was marched past the reviewing admiral after the awarding of 'wings'. Though appreciative of the efforts being made on my behalf, I resolved I would not risk letting my naval friends down. So, when the great day came, I shuffled up to the dais to receive my wings, watched rather disapprovingly by the reviewing admiral who, after fixing my wings on, tartly observed, 'Now, Doctor, I suppose you'll want to be getting back to your chosen profession', rather in the tones of 'England expects ...' To his astonishment and my relief, a medical orderly came up and informed me that my presence in the sick-bay would be appreciated as soon as possible. Little did he know that this was part of a scurrilous and rather unethical plan to avoid my having to take part in the subsequent march-past!

After Yatesbury and Kirton-in-Lindsey we were handed

back to the Navy to complete our training. It was impressed upon us that our newly awarded naval wings were provisional only, and whether we kept them or not depended on whether we successfully completed the eight deck landings which were obligatory at that time. This part of the training was done at the naval air station at Lossiemouth, in Firefly aircraft for the old gentlemen such as myself, and Seafires for the rest.

The course pilots, after becoming familiar with the Firefly aircraft they were training on, were encouraged to take their fellow pilots up as passengers in the rear seat. This seat had no controls and only a limited view. The idea did not appeal to me. My fellow doctor, Fin Lennan, elected to fly with me, and the trip passed off uneventfully. I felt honour-bound to return the compliment, but with misgivings. Fin would be the first to agree that, whilst being a very good doctor, his flying of an aeroplane was about as natural a relationship as an elephant riding a bicycle. My misgivings increased when I learned that my flight with Fin was to be part of a huge formation fly-past for the benefit of a visiting admiral.

I had never liked formation flying; moreover, it was a gusty, windy day. I pulled my safety harness particularly tight as we waited to take off. The 'balbo' of aircraft formed into some sort of order before zooming to and fro before the admiral, and I could make out the small group of visitors standing in front of the control tower holding on to their hats. The wind had increased! Came the time to land. First time round, Fin wasn't satisfied with his approach (nor was I!), abandoned it and slowly climbed away. 'Good man!' I said over the 'intercom', relieved at having just missed the lighthouse on the Lossiemouth golf course just short of the runway. I also noticed two golfers running – I did not associate golfers with running. Round we went for another approach. This time the lighthouse appeared on the *other* side of the aircraft, and off we went again.

I noticed by this time that all the other aircraft had apparently landed. Fin was giving an individual flying display, with me as an unwilling participant.

I felt lonely, for I could not see my pilot but could hear him muttering, 'Undercarriage, flaps, pitch …' as we turned downwind for the third attempt. This time, as we turned onto the approach, I could see the lighthouse way below and the golfers with white, upturned faces. I returned their frightened gazes – we were much too high. I heard the engine noise die away and we descended like a lift out of control, to hit the runway with a thud. I saw the undercarriage wheels passing my window as the struts collapsed, followed by a cartwheeling manoeuvre – wing, propeller, wing – before settling, fortunately, upright. As I struggled to undo my harness, a figure flashed by my window. Fin on his way to the bar, I thought. Then, moments later, the same figure flashed by again, onto the wing, leaned into the front cockpit, plugged in his intercom and said, 'Terribly sorry, old boy. It's time to get out', then flashed by again. This time I was not far behind.

This was but one of many similar incidents which occurred about this time, with the aircraft then in service. For one reason or another, no fewer than five pilots lost their lives from No. 8 course, which produced only three pilots for front-line squadron service.

Towards the end of the course at Lossiemouth a carrier was despatched to the Moray Firth to allow us to try our luck at deck landing. It was a moot point as to which party was the more nervous, the students or the ship's air department.

One pilot, Mike Fanshawe, overshot the arrester wires and disappeared in a plume of spray into the sea over the bows of the training carrier *Illustrious*. He recalls hearing the ominous thudding of the ship's screws passing over him before emerging from his aircraft and surfacing, only to see the bows of the following destroyer bearing down upon him ('Oh no … not again'). He was eventually picked up and was lucky to escape with a fractured femur. My professional colleague Fin Lennan 'bent' two aircraft in five attempts to land on the ship and was given an 'Honorary Degree' in deck landing but strict instructions never to put his training into practice!

The experience left me with the conclusion that there was scope for a considerable amount of improvement.

Flying training completed, the Naval Medical Department, which had not whole-heartedly approved one of their ilk taking to the air, thought fit to appoint me as medical officer to HMS *Vengeance*, a light fleet-carrier at that time undergoing a refit in dry dock at Rosyth. The significance of this escaped me at first for I had been taught nothing of the protocol of getting 'on' and 'off' HM ships. My indoctrination course at Chatham had not thought this necessary. I arrived at Rosyth late one night when everyone had gone either home or to bed, and thus walked aboard with the minimum of ceremony. The ship was like HMS *Victory* – in dry dock!

The next morning I was greeted in a fatherly but firm way by the Commander, who had no fewer than five decorations for his war-time achievements in submarines and who resented his latest appointment to an aircraft-carrier, where submergence at sea would be *most* inappropriate. 'Get to know the proper drill before I catch you going ashore; when and whom to salute; order of seniority in boats, and when and whom to salute when returning on board.' I felt, and was, trapped.

For the next two weeks, whilst the ship completed its refit, I contrived to proceed 'ashore' at inconspicuous times, after dark and in plain clothes, thus avoiding a confrontation with the 'Spirit of Nelson'.

Inevitably the time came when the lock gates were opened and the sea rushed into the dry dock. *Vengeance* was floated into the tideway and tied up to a buoy in the main channel. The ship's daily routine was followed, including ceremonial events: colours, sunset, saluting the quarterdeck. It took me a long time to identify the quarterdeck in a carrier, for it was marked only by a strip of brass. Once I had identified it, I spent a lot of time surreptitiously crossing it, usually after dark, until I felt I had mastered a sufficiently nonchalant salute to avoid comment. For the most part I spent my time scurrying along dark alleyways between my cabin, the sick-bay and the wardroom; all enclosed spaces. I felt a bond between myself and a particularly large rat which lived on top of the ventilation trunking in the wardroom. He was clearly visible, watching us with his red eyes and blatantly regarding the officers with contempt. The ventilation trunking system provided him with suitable access round the ship. To me, as a land-lubber, he even appeared to give a form of salute as he entered the wardroom along the trunking, though in retrospect he was probably just scratching his nose.

During the next two weeks I accepted that the only way ashore lay by way of the ships' boat calling at the ship's *port* after gangway. One abortive attempt to board a boat at the *starboard* after gangway left me in no doubt that this was reserved for captains and admirals. I could not see any way of attaining this in the short term; in any case, the comings and goings of such exalted ranks were inevitably accompanied by cries of 'Man the side!' followed by piercing shrieks on a bosun's pipe rather like a train guard's whistle. (This should not be confused with another old naval term, 'Man overboard!' though each cry creates a similar amount of excitement.) I abandoned my immediate plans for going ashore till I knew more about what was involved. For some days I peered out of my scuttle (I was learning the jargon), which was conveniently situated directly above the point where the boat would pull alongside the carrier. All I could observe was a ritual of physical jerks by sailors performing a ballet with a boathook as they approached the ship. On one occasion an over-enthusiastic rating fell in at the very place where the ship's effluent discharged. The water being suspect, I was summoned to the sick-bay to confirm his fitness to continue duties. By subtle questioning of the unfortunate man, I gleaned quite a bit about what went on at these times.

Watching the boat drill did little to help my cause except to allow me to note that there was, as at Chatham Barracks, a close season around nine o'clock in the morning, at colours, and at sunset, when bugles sounded and everyone had to stand to attention facing a certain direction – rather like Muslims, I reflected. If caught in a small boat during this ceremony, I didn't think the risk of falling into the sea could be justified and I again spent the next week on board. Sanity and a desire to re-establish my freedom eventually prevailed but there was still the boat drill to overcome in getting from ship to shore. I had been warned darkly that to get in and out of a boat other than in strict order of seniority was a social gaff, if not actually invoking the Naval Discipline Act. This order seemed to reverse depending on whether entering or leaving the boat. I was non-plussed. I could only guess that the reason for this ritual was to enable senior officers to reach the bar ahead of the crowd or to spend the shortest possible time in small boats in case they succumbed to sea-sickness. Unless one carried an up-to-date copy of the Navy List, wherever one went one would clearly soon be in trouble.

I spent a further miserable three weeks whilst we underwent various tests, including full power trials, when the ship resembled an expensive form of vibro-massage, followed by listing trials, when everything fell out of the lockers, gin out of glasses etc, before we were pronounced fit to receive aircraft aboard. My spirits perked up. I awaited the time for embarkation of our first squadron of Seafires with some anticipation. It seemed a long time since I had done my flying training, and I was finding my sick-bay duties rather dull by contrast.

The day we embarked our aircraft was eventful on three counts.

First, the second aircraft to arrive failed to engage our arrester wire and tangled itself in the safety barrier. I felt this to be careless as well as expensive.

Secondly, my cabin was immediately beneath the flight deck, and I had taken to hanging my newly washed drip-dry shirt on a hawser-like wire stretching from one side of my cabin to the other, conveniently and thoughtfully placed, I reflected at the time, across the deck head. Whilst in my cabin I was astonished to hear a whine and, simultaneously, see my newly laundered shirt suddenly rush across the cabin and disappear from view into a hole. I never saw it again. I learned to my cost that my 'clothes line' was an arrester wire and that the incident signified the arrival of another aircraft.

The third incident of that day came after the aircraft had landed. I observed that, once safely on board and parked for'ard on the flight deck, the pilot would clamber out of his aircraft with all possible speed and a minimum of ceremony and make his way to the interior of the ship. This dispensed with all the normal practice of saluting with deference to seniority etc. I resolved that, whenever possible, I would arrive and leave His Majesty's ships by courtesy of the air service so thoughtfully provided. I had my wings and I would use them.

3 *'Joining Circuit, Farnborough'*

It was a beautiful autumn day in 1949. HMS *Vengeance* was lying at anchor at Spithead. I had served as the ship's medical officer for nearly a year and was wondering if I would ever fulfil my ambition of furthering my flying career. After my flying course and gaining my wings I had been told to be patient and 'get some time in'. I did not feel cut out to spend the rest of my Service days diagnosing and treating the various relatively simple ailments contracted by sailors and was growing impatient.

On this cloudless morning I had come up to the flight deck for some fresh air. The sun was still low down when I saw the ship's commanding officer, Captain John Cuthbert, telescope tucked under his arm, on the other side of the flight deck making his way to the bridge; we were to put to sea within the hour to embark our squadrons of Fireflies and Seafuries. I saw him glancing towards me repeatedly and I suddenly realized I should salute him, as was the custom when one met one's commanding officer for the first time in the morning. I also realized that he could not possibly have seen any mark of respect I might have paid as I was directly up sun. It was a classic Catch 22 situation that I continually found myself in but, as so often happened, honour was saved by the compelling sound of 'colours' and we *both* saluted as we faced aft whilst the White Ensign was duly hoisted. The ceremony completed, he said, 'Ah, Doctor, I wanted to see you; you're to go on a jet conversion course, and then you'll be appointed to Farnborough, to the RAF Institute of Aviation Medicine.'

I was stunned, then euphoric.

At that time jets were still something of a novel way of getting airborne, and the Navy had yet to form its first operational jet squadron. I felt that I was participating in a transformation as great as the change from sails to steam. If the views of some of the old sea-dogs who had not had the benefit of carrier service was anything to go by, the experience was to be just as traumatic. The dwindling though still influential number of such senior officers were entrenched around the last of the great battleships – *Vanguard* was shortly to pay off and be put into reserve – and a shrinking number of cruisers still left in commission. Thus, if these sea-dogs wanted to be given command of a sea-going ship, they had to bury their pride and accept appointment to a 'flat top'. I overheard one such senior captain, on assuming command, observe that it was akin to driving a crab (he had been a submariner) and, to my surprise, when giving a young RNVR pilot a ticking off – no doubt deserved – finished by telling him, 'Remember, you might be *in* the Navy but you're not *of* the Navy.'

To be fair, such officers, many of whom served in the era of the 'Grand Fleet' and had seen the Fleet Air Arm enter the war in 1939 with a mere 218 aircraft, soon altered their views after a few weeks at sea operating their relatively primitive aircraft. (Fully described by Geoffrey Till in his book *Air Power and the Royal Navy: 1914-1945* Jane's Publishing Co., 1979).

As a measure of the hazards and difficulties of landing the Seafires, Seafuries, Firebrands and similar aircraft in the immediate post-war period, one landing in eighty-eight aboard a carrier resulted in some sort of material damage. The position was to change radically, if paradoxically, with the advent of higher-performance jet aircraft and the introduction of new techniques.

Group Captain Pat Ruffell Smith and his son Hugh

Captain I.G.W. Robertson, last commanding officer of HMS *Eagle* (1970–2)

The experimental prone position Meteor

Sea Hawk naval fighter – autographed by Hawker's chief test pilot, Neville Duke. The earlier production models were not pressurised, an expensive policy omission

I was put ashore at Penzance and reported to the Royal Naval Air Station at Culdrose, near the Lizard. One of the few naval pilots qualified in jets, Lieutenant 'Nobby' Clark, greeted me and handed me over to Lieutenant Pete Perrett to be introduced to the delights of flying jets.

In 1949 the RAF had several operational jet aircraft squadrons but the Navy was quite a long way behind. 700 Squadron at Culdrose had just been formed. Its purpose was to give initial jet experience to naval aviators, and it was equipped with a dual-controlled Meteor 7 and a few Vampire aircraft. The Navy was awakening and catching up. The advent of the jet era meant a sudden leap forward in aircraft performance which outstripped human ability to withstand unaided the reduced atmospheric pressures at operational jet altitudes. Considerable acceleration forces and high speeds all necessitated further adaptation of equipment to protect aircrew operating over the sea and from ships. A whole new world was waiting to be explored from a physiological standpoint.

The next few weeks passed rapidly and enjoyably, and at the end I was pronounced fit to fly jets and received my appointment to HMS *President* for duties at the RAF Institute of Aviation Medicine, Farnborough and as Naval Medical Liaison Officer.* The wording of the appointment stated nothing but meant everything. In plain words, 'What you do or make of the job is up to you.' A report of progress had to be made twice a year to the Department of the Medical Director General (Naval).

So, one beautiful May day in 1950 my wife, Margaret, and I found ourselves two furnished rooms in the Old Rectory at Farnham, not many miles from Farnborough,

* In order to be paid, naval officers have to be appointed to a ship. HMS *President* can still be seen alongside the Thames Embankment, London, and the vessel is used for training purposes, including the Royal Naval Reserve. It is, in theory, also used to receive appointments, such as mine, which cannot conveniently be fitted in anywhere else and is purely for purposes of administration.

the focal point of all that was new in aviation. The next day, leaving Margaret to find a more permanent home, I drove to the Royal Aircraft Establishment at Farnborough in our old Ford 'Popular'. Being so far from the sea, I felt like a fish out of water, sporting my naval uniform with its two gold rings with red in between, signifying I was a naval surgeon, although it was also surmounted by pilot's wings on my left sleeve.

To say I felt nervous would be an understatement. How was I, with my lack of experience, to fit in with the professionals at Farnborough? They were, after all, the leading exponents of developmental flying and were backed up by the very best aerodynamicists at the RAE and the specialist physiologists at the RAF Institute of Aviation Medicine.

In these years of the late 1940s and early 1950s, with the dozen or so independent aircraft manufacturers vying with each other to obtain Government contracts for their aircraft, prototypes were pushed to their design limits and often beyond, in the race to break existing altitude and speed records. Farnborough was synonymous with experimental flying. Hardly a week passed without reference being made on the BBC to a British prototype either making a maiden flight or crashing. Very often the pilot was killed. Increasingly, however, it was announced that the pilot had been saved by using his Martin-Baker ejection seat.

It was against this background that I drove through the security gate and was directed, with an escort, to the RAF Institute of Aviation Medicine. Throughout there was the hum of jet engines setting the scene.

I was met at the door of the Institute by 'Happy' Day, the janitor, a dour civil servant who, I was later to learn, knew more about the thirty-odd medical officers at Farnborough than anyone else. He was the archetypical 'odd job man' so often found in these quasi-academic establishments; he effectively held the place together. He would appear from nowhere, usually holding a piece of oxygen tubing in one hand and a spanner in the other. For the thirty eccentric doctors and scientists, with an element of the prima donna in them, 'Happy' Day provided a safety valve. If a piece of equipment went wrong or was lost, it was 'Happy' who managed to sort out the problem.

While I waited, I took stock of my surroundings. The 'Lab' consisted of a two-storey building standing on a hill overlooking the main Farnborough airfield. It had a number of offshoots which, I learned later, were to house the centrifuge, the climatic laboratory and the other blocks where human experiments were carried out. The main runway was just visible, and beyond, an untidy collection of factory buildings which represented the Royal Aircraft Establishment. The scene could have belonged to the early years of the century and was relieved only by a modern air-traffic control tower. To the right of the runway, protected by iron railings, was the stump of a tree, 'Cody's tree', where that aviation pioneer was reported to have tethered his early flying-machine. I picked out the silhouette of the 'black shed' so beloved by commentators when identifying aircraft flying at the Society of British Aircraft Constructors show. I noticed a vertical trellis-like structure sticking up from behind the black shed, perhaps twenty-five feet in height. As I watched, a figure shot up the structure, apparently sitting on a seat, and came to a halt near the top. He was clearly alive for he was gesticulating to those on the ground beneath him. A few seconds later I heard a muffled explosion and realized that I was watching a simulated ejection from an aircraft on the experimental rig. It was on this rig that Air Vice-Marshal W.K. Stewart did much of the early work on how the body responds to acceleration. Bill Stewart was the doyen of aviation medicine and held in high esteem as an authority on both sides of the Atlantic.

My view was interrupted by an unusual aircraft coming in to land. Jet propelled, it was shaped like a boomerang with no fuselage or 'body' and no tail. A vertical fin projected from the tip of each wing and, apart from the undercarriage, nothing else broke the continuous line of the 'flying wing'. It was an experimental aerodynamic shape built by Armstrong Whitworth, but it never progressed beyond the prototype stage.

Reality returned when I heard my name called by 'Happy' Day and I was led in to be welcomed by the commandant, Wing Commander W.K. Stewart.

Until the late 1930s the needs of pilots remained relatively simple and largely unrecognized. A leather jacket, a pair of goggles and a scarf tended to be the popular image of the 'magnificent men in their flying-machines', an image left over from the First World War.

There were, however, one or two disconcerting stories. The Schneider Trophy pilots noticed a dimming of vision as they pulled tight turns round the triangular course. A few lone voices were beginning to observe that some serious research would be required into human physiological needs for the new generation of monoplanes that were to form the backbone of Britain's air defences. By the time the war had begun in earnest and battle had been joined between the Spitfires, Hurricanes and Heinkels, some problem areas had become apparent:

Need for Oxygen: The physiologists were able to demonstrate this was necessary for effective performance above 10,000 feet, and if full night vision was required, above 4,000 feet.

Night Vision: The British public soon took to eating their quota of carrots to keep up their Vitamin A intake and so emulate the night-fighter pilots who found that carrots improved their vision. After the cessation of hostilities in World War II, cynics suggested that this was a propaganda story put about by the Government. The purpose (it was said) was to blind the Germans from the real secret of successful night vision – the introduction of radar. Be this true or not, the medical fact is that, without adequate Vitamin A, night vision deteriorates – perhaps a good example of the propaganda maxim 'Be economical with the truth without actually lying'.

Clothing: This needed special development as the early aircraft were not pressurized and as heating was inadequate.

Life-Jackets: There was a need to support an unconscious pilot at an angle of forty-five degrees face upwards; otherwise, like a bottle floating vertically, he would submerge. As an example of the thoroughness of the research, Dr Pask had himself anaesthetized and 'floated' in a tank to remove any possibility of involuntary movement whilst conscious.

Blacking Out: Methods of compressing limbs and abdomen were devised to restore the blood circulation to the brain whilst involved in 'tight turns' during manoeuvres.

Aircrew Morale It was a measure of how little this problem was understood that the term 'lack of moral fibre' (LMF) was able to gain recognition at all.

By the end of the war, aircraft performance had advanced to a degree at which pilots were disadvantaged unless supported by special equipment. The emphasis had changed from basic to applied research. From helping the human body to adapt to a hostile environment, it was now necessary to modify that environment so as to enable the human body not only to survive but to operate effectively and efficiently.

I believe the foundations for successful research at the Institute of Aviation Medicine lay in the spirit of questioning innovation pursued by the 'lab's' founder, Dr (later Sir) Bryan Matthews CBE, MA, FRS, DSc, at the beginning of World War II, when he was prised out from his retreat at Cambridge to continue his research into oxygen problems. This time he was to direct his enquiries into the needs of aircrew, rather than activities in the Andes, as hitherto. He gathered a staff of four in a small lean-to shed at the Royal Aircraft Establishment, Farnborough, all for the princely salary of £500 per annum. The 'Lab' was born.

On one issue, however, Matthews was adamant. He would not be coerced into uniform – he would remain a civilian, and so he did throughout the war. By so doing he doubtless retained a freedom of action which might have been denied to him had he submitted to a form of discipline which was anathema to him. This freedom of action which Matthews retained set the hallmark of the Lab and later the Institute of Aviation Medicine, enabling the medical pilots to have access to aeroplanes and techniques not normally available to non-experimental service pilots.

Matthews' researches soon required him to take to the air and, though not a qualified pilot himself, he gained a lot of knowledge of flying-skills in the process, playing his part in the operating of the aircraft during flying.

A story which Matthews himself likes to recall tells of the time when he was asked by the Director of RAF Medical Services, Air Marshal Sir Harold Whittingham KCB, KBE, to visit the Second Tactical Air Force in Germany at the end of the war. Matthews was told he would need to don uniform for security reasons. This part of the proposal did not appeal to him, for he regarded uniform as a symbol of captivity and with the greatest of suspicion. Whittingham pointed out that Churchill had taken to wearing the uniform of an Air Commodore when travelling in RAF aircraft, and if the Prime Minister was willing, then surely it was not unreasonable to ask that the

Director of the Institute should do the same. It so happened that, not long before, Churchill had visited Farnborough to be fitted out with a specially adapted oxygen mask to enable him to smoke his cigar whilst flying at medium altitude on long journeys, so Whittingham won the day. It is no mean tribute to Matthews' bargaining strength that it was agreed that he too should wear the rank of an Air Commodore!

Wing Commander Pat Ruffell Smith, an RAF doctor who had piloted Matthews on many of his experimental flights, elected to fly him to Germany in a Beaufighter, and it was left to Matthews to be in charge of the navigational side.

Since he had not worn uniform before, a short training programme was arranged to acquaint him as to the niceties and protocol likely to be encountered during the trip. He presented a somewhat unorthodox figure, wearing an Air Commodore's broad stripe, a neat but most un-regulation clipped moustache, with piercing eyes, surmounted by a cap with two rows of gold braid, perched uncertainly and somewhat awkwardly on his head. It was mutually agreed after a few forays across open ground that walking, and certainly marching, should be kept to a minimum for fear of giving the game away. A few lessons in raising his *right* hand at an appropriate angle to his cap eventually produced a gesture that could pass for a salute if required, and they were ready to set off for Germany towards the end of the day. Matthews told me the story as follows:

'I had learned sufficient about navigating to be able to advise my pilot how to get from A to B to C and back again around the South of England and felt confident that I could direct my Doctor pilot to Wiesbaden in Germany. I had not, however, made such a long flight in one direction before and I forgot to allow for the fact that the sun sets somewhat earlier the further East one travelled. Thus by the time we arrived in the vicinity of our destination it was completely dark, and no runway lights were available. However, with the aid of numerous Verey lights being fired, Pat found the airfield and made a perfect landing.'

Perhaps it was a fortunate mistake, for it enabled Matthews to arrive under cover of darkness, calling for the minimum of protocol and saluting and exposure to critical eyes. The crowning glory came later, in the officers' mess, when an erstwhile colleague of Matthews at Cambridge, now enlisted in the RAF as a flight lieutenant, approached him diffidently and respectfully, explaining he shouldn't really be seen talking to such a distinguished senior officer.

And so the pattern was laid for later years. The ability to cut through red tape enabled experiments to be carried out drawing upon modern aeroplanes, many of them prototypes, and often assistance was offered from unexpected quarters.

In the late 1940s what had been known as the Physiology Laboratory became the RAF Institute of Aviation Medicine. Research into the special needs of Navy flying, on the other hand, continued to be investigated by naval medical officers, some of whom had air experience and one or two of whom were qualified pilots. However, the emphasis was on survival at sea and in the sea, leaving most of the applied aviation medical research to the RAF team at Farnborough. The limited naval research was conducted at the Royal Navy Air Medical School, where the main task was to train naval air crew about the physiological aspects of flying naval aircraft.

By the late 1940s a considerable amount of the applied research at Farnborough was carried out in aircraft adapted for the purpose. Credit for the inauguration and development of airborne experimentation must be given to Group Captain Pat Ruffell Smith. Pat was unique among medical pilots. He had a flair for seeing the hazards lying far beyond the immediate problems. He could see that the time had arrived when the design of the aircraft had to recognize pilots' limitations. No longer would it suffice to wrap aircrew up in appropriate clothing and issue them with goggles to protect eyes, and a scarf for good measure; a microphone was later added to shout 'tally ho' (the accepted war-cry), interspersed with a few well-chosen words – 'wizard prang', 'press-on' etc; the handlebar moustache completed the image. Aeroplanes were becoming sophisticated, and Pat Ruffell Smith was determined that pilots should match them, backed up with hardware rather than war-cries.

It was not until I had been at Farnborough for some time that I was to learn of the Lab's early beginnings and the part that Pat Ruffell Smith had played in getting the practical flying side established and accepted.

When I first arrived at Farnborough, what I lacked in experience I made up with enthusiasm. It was Pat who, quite properly, kept that enthusiasm in check. On first meeting him he appeared rather distant and aloof. To me, as a young surgeon lieutenant, he was an elderly wing commander doctor, rather like a don in uniform, with 'wings' and rows of medals, both British and foreign. (One of them looked as though it had a bumble bee in the middle of the ribbon – I found out later that it was the Polish Virtute Militori and had been awarded to Pat for looking after Polish aircrew in the war.)

I was impatient. I had completed my flying course, obtained the basic instrument rating, qualified on light 'twins' and converted onto jets (at this time an almost unknown method of propulsion in the Navy). I was keen to show off my paces, and my impatience grew as I felt frustrated at being – apparently – held back by this awesome RAF doctor pilot, eternally smoking a pipe, who seemed equally at home in anything from a Lancaster bomber to a modern jet. Only later did I learn that it had taken many years of planning – and of pleading with and even threatening, in a veiled way, the powers in the Air Ministry – to allow him to have selected aircraft specifically allocated for airborne medical research.

One of these aircraft, not often flown, I noted, was a Spitfire Mark 22, one of the last of its line, with the powerful Griffon engine. The only use it was put to was an occasional sortie to test 'G-suits',* garments which looked like a cross between Victorian ladies' corsets and bishops' gaiters. I did not fancy being dressed up like a hermaphrodite but was desperate to do more flying, so I professed a sudden interest in the mysteries of acceleration and how to combat it, and was given permission to continue the evaluation of G-suits.

Having studied the pilot's notes, I hobbled out to the Spitfire, wearing my newly issued 'underwear' for my indoctrination sortie. I knew that, if I was to be accepted at the Lab, I had to express undying love and devotion for this over-powered and lusty machine, which I certainly didn't feel. I persevered, conspicuously waddling around the Lab in my ungainly 'gaiters', even turning up at coffee breaks making sure everyone knew what I was doing, before struggling into the old war-horse, which I nearly began to love, and pushing it noisily around the Hampshire skies in ever-tightening turns. As the G forces built up, my vision would pale, before the acceleration-sensitive G-valve opened, pumping air into the bladders built into the suit, giving a punch in the stomach more appropriate to a boxing ring but restoring one's failing senses. It was as dramatic as turning on a light as the

* G is the unit of the Earth's gravitational field. The force exerted on a pilot flying an aircraft in a tight turn is expressed in units of G – 2G, 4G etc. The effect on a pilot is to drain the blood into the dependent 'soft' parts of the body, such as the abdomen and the legs. Thus the brain is deprived of its blood-supply causing first loss of vision, then unconciousness. Hearing is the last sense to be lost. A G-suit consists of bladders, applied to the abdomen and legs which fill with air under such conditions, applying a counter-pressure in an attempt to force the blood back to the brain.

blood flowed back to the brain. I began to make some practical suggestions for alleviating the severity of the punch in the solar plexus, by slowing down the rate of opening of the G-valve.

It seemed only fair that some of the 'boffins' should experience the benefit of their own designing, and I persuaded Pat to have a G-valve installed in the Lab dual-controlled Meteor. By the twinkle in Pat's eyes it was apparent that he felt he had a willing pupil. For my part I was keen to share the joys of my airborne 'massage parlour' with others.

When the Meteor was fitted up, I encouraged – nay, compelled – the 'boffins' to accompany me on many G-loaded sorties and I developed something of a reputation as an airborne anaesthetist, by the simple expediency of having my passenger's G-valve set to open slightly later than my own. Thus I retained consciousness, whilst my passengers were despatched, by the manoeuvre, into a light doze due to blood draining from the brain. I won a quite unwarranted reputation for having a very high G threshold!

My predecessor on the Spitfire project, Johnny Howitt, thought this most unfair. To give him credit, he had done the bulk of the G-suit development work and flew many hours in the course of his dedicated experimental flying. I suspect that he spent a good deal more of his airborne time in excess of 5G than below it. It was said of him, on his moving to another appointment, that he had arrived at Farnborough a spritely twenty-six-year-old doctor and left four years later as a middle-aged consultant.

I found, following these experiments, that I had become accepted by Pat. I felt that my baptism by (Spit)fire had not been in vain.

Pat possessed another essential quality: he knew how to plan a campaign against 'them', as he called the influential but dogmatic and often ageing, pilots in the Air Ministry. He used cunning but invariably legitimate ploys to achieve his ends. He was no amateur when it came to politics.

Wing Commander Tony Barwood, an RAF doctor, was working on an air-ventilated flying-unit for use in tropical conditions, where aircrew might have to exist in the aircraft, on the ground, for long periods without adequate cooling facilities. Tony's experimentation had reached a stage where he needed to put his work to the test in a Vampire. He was in despair trying to achieve this end when Pat called into his office with a letter written to the Air Ministry above Tony's name, and asked him to append his signature. Tony was mildly surprised to read a brief but very technical essay on the 'pathogenesis of hypernatraemia'. Interspersed in the technical terms such as 'increased solute ouput' and 'reduced maximum osmolality of the urine leading to hyper-osmolar coma' were more recognizable lay terms like 'renal failure'. Towards the end of this very erudite paper came the clear warning that such conditions could well come about whilst operating aircraft with perspex canopies in tropical conditions, especially if those aircraft were manned on a stand-by basis on the ground. It was recommended that tropical trials be expedited using the air-ventilated suit being developed at Farnborough.

Tony got his trials undertaken in the Lab Vampire shortly afterwards at Khartoum.

Pat had a puckish sense of humour which he employed to good effect when dealing with civil servants. With a little encouragement he clearly derived much satisfaction in recounting an early experience in his career.

Before World War II, doctors were encouraged to join the Services on a five-year short-service commission, at the end of which they were given a gratuity of £1,000 – unless they transferred to a regular commission, in which case the gratuity was not payable. Pat took such a commission, and his five years were completed during the war. He was paid his £1,000 but was retained in uniform along with all other wartime officers.

At the end of the war he was accepted for a regular commission and, in due course, received a letter asking him to repay his £1,000, which he declined to do, reasoning that he had completed his side of the bargain and had been prepared to be discharged, had he been allowed. He was eventually summoned to a 'high civil servant' (he was of sufficient seniority that he had a carpet and a hat-stand in his room, which impressed Pat). For half an hour the civil servant argued and tried to persuade Pat that he must repay the £1,000, but to no avail. The interview clearly coming to an unsuccessful end (from the civil servant's standpoint), he rose to his feet and, leading Pat by the arm out of his office, firmly closed the door and said, 'And don't you pay a penny of that gratuity back – you're entitled to it.'

Which all goes to say that even civil servants can be human.

4 *Fly Like a Bird ...*

Since the beginning of time, man has envied birds their ability to take to the air and has watched, studied and attempted to imitate them, to no avail. Man eventually took to the air in his own way, in a contraption with propellers and wings which were fixed or rotary but certainly not flapping.

It would, however, be unwise to assume that we have little to learn from our ornithological friends. There is a passing similarity between the sight of a jumbo jet coming in to land, with a mass of flaps hanging down, bunches of aircraft wheels stretching for the earth like claws, and a snow goose arriving at its winter base after a long trans-oceanic crossing. The Red Arrows in Gnats (later Hawks) move around in tight circles like a covey of partridge. Watch a duck come in low for an anticipated landing on a lake only to find, on touching down, that the 'landing strip' is frozen. Instead of taking off again, as human pilots are trained to do, it attempts to bring into play the ornithological equivalent of 'reverse thrust' as it slithers and tumbles along the icy runway.

Take-offs in the feathered world can be fraught with problems calling for initiative. This was apparent one Christmas when I was visiting Slimbridge Wildfowl Trust, in Gloucestershire, and standing in the picture-window drawing-room overlooking the crowded lake. There was a lot of 'traffic' around the lake: birds of varying size were wheeling overhead lining up to land on the busy surface. A swan was seeking a clearway to start his take-off run, paddling slowly to and fro along the down-wind bank of the pond. One could almost see his frustration as, thrusting his beak hither and thither, he suddenly turned into the wind and commenced take-off, spreading his wings, neck outstretched and exerting every bit of power he possessed. He had almost reached V2 (rotate) when a water hen paddled slowly across his take-off path. He couldn't rotate, nor would it have been dignified to abandon his take-off. He didn't hesitate but, rather like a soldier changing step, lifted one leg up and stepped over the surprised water hen. A moment later he was airborne and away.

It was with such thoughts as these that I first came to Farnborough. My brief was a simple one and implied in the term of my appointment – 'Naval Medical Liaison Officer'. I knew I was privileged to be working alongside a rather special, if not assertive team of doctors, mostly RAF. Many of them had other qualifications apart from medical degrees: one had an engineering degree and was involved in the mechanics of pressure suits; another had a science degree and specialized in the mathematical mysteries of acceleration and its effects on the body. But it was to the small group of flying doctors that I was attracted, with their privileged access to the new generation of high-performance aircraft, many of them still in experimental stages. I had been cautioned not to be impatient, but to 'observe' – in other words: to speak only when I was spoken to. I felt the interpretation of the 'silent service' could be carried too far. I remembered my father's advice to me in another context when I was a small boy, with a tendency to burst out with some new-found excitement. He said, 'When you enter a room, or new environment, go in quietly and weigh up the atmosphere before speaking. Match your words to that atmosphere and you will be the better accepted.'

I watched and listened patiently, and the more I observed, the more inadequate I felt, except that I was qualified to fly an aeroplane.

However, my father had taught me something else which stood me in good stead at this stage in my life. When I was growing up and, like many adolescents, inclined to shyness, I hated going into a crowded room. He would tell me to remember that, however august the persons in the room might be, there would be something that I would be able to do better than anyone else in the room. At Farnborough I needed to fall back on this piece of wisdom, for it seemed to me that the thirty doctors there were all tarred with the brush of genius in some way or another – and with the eccentricity that usually goes with it. But with few exceptions they couldn't fly and, knowing my willingness, they used me as an airborne taxi-driver – to get to bases, many of them in out-of-the-way places, or to try their sometimes bizarre ideas in the air, and gradually I was accepted, even though my dark blue uniform against the RAF light blue underlined me as an erstwhile fish out of water.

In a short while my plea for further support was successful, and I was joined by a fellow naval medical officer, John Rawlins, (later to become Surgeon Vice-Admiral, Medical Director General of the Royal Navy), who, though not a qualified aviator, was well equipped intellectually to keep our end up, for inter-Service rivalry was not unheard-of even in the scientific backwater of Farnborough.

By the early 1950s the strategic limits to high-altitude flying were being probed, and a new concept was being bandied about along the lines of flying as fast and as low as possible, primarily to avoid detection by enemy radar. To meet this requirement the TSR 2 was designed, though later to be scrapped in one of the periodic Defence cuts, shortly after its maiden flight.

Two main problems came from high-speed low-level

flying: the difficulty of visual navigation recognizing topographical landmarks as they flashed by, and the severe physical buffeting suffered by both aircraft and crew from low-level turbulence.

Ingenious efforts to overcome the navigational difficulties resulted in the 'rolling map' which was prepared along a pre-determined flight path and unwound from one spool to another (like a camera film) driven by an electric motor linked to the aircraft's speed. A refinement of this was the 'audio map' giving the pilot a pre-recorded commentary on the main topographical features he should look for.

The buffeting was a different matter. At speeds in excess of 500 mph the initial experimental task was to fly as close as possible to the ground and just see what happened. For short familiarization experience we would use the west-to-east runway of Farnborough itself, coming in low over open heathland giving a gentle downhill run onto the main runway and coming to within two or three feet of the surface. For the first time I realized that the runway had 'hills' in it, which required flying 'over'.

We had a 'set' route from Farnborough to Lulworth Cove and back, for which we used the Lab's Meteor 7. However, in spite of making every effort to avoid not only populated areas but even individual dwellings, it became evident that some disturbance was inevitably being caused to members of the population, so our experimental runs were transferred to North Africa, where we had the benefit of even greater turbulence caused by air rising from the hot desert sand. Living now in semi-retirement in an isolated, sleepy village in the Cotswolds, I often look up as a low-flying Phantom or Tornado tears overhead on a training mission. I know only too well that the greatest care is taken to minimize disturbance and annoyance to the population as well as animals. Furthermore, 'low flying' today is measured in hundreds of feet rather than the tens of feet of our experimental flying.

It was astonishing to find the damage which the buffeting inflicted on the aircraft – rivets would 'pop' out, just as the heat tiles came off during the early flights of the American Space Shuttle. The aircraft were closely inspected after each sortie, which lasted about forty minutes, by which time the aircraft had exhausted its fuel due to a combination of the high speed and low-level flying. The frequency and magnitude of the aircraft buffeting were carefully recorded to see if there was any relationship between them and the natural resonating frequencies of various parts of the human body. This could and did occur on occasions, and further laboratory experiments were set up (described in Chapter 13). In the meantime, ways of absorbing the more 'threatening' frequencies were evolved. These, in the main, consisted of inserting 'deadening' materials in the 'biscuit' or cushion on which the pilot sat whilst flying, so preventing certain oscillating frequencies being passed into the pilot's body.

I became increasingly interested in the more direct skills of high-speed low flying. To alter course, albeit by as little as ten or twenty degrees at speeds of 500 knots or so, necessitated applying as much as eighty-five degrees of 'bank' if one was not to get hopelessly lost and a long way off course. I noticed that other pilots as well as myself would pull up 200-300 feet before executing a sharp turn, and this manoeuvre would, of course, mean revealing oneself to 'enemy' radar, thus losing the element of surprise in staying close to the ground – even when in a steep banking turn.

I pondered on this for several weeks. I noticed when following cars on the road that some drivers, usually young women or drivers sporting L plates, would 'lean' inwards on going round a corner, whereas 'older' drivers kept their heads upright. I also noticed that these leaning drivers tended to steer a more erratic course round bends, as compared with older drivers. It seemed that there must be a correlation with our low-flying problem in going round corners. I found myself covertly following young girls going round corners in cars. I noticed that they 'leaned' their heads inwards only when going round corners fast. When turning slowly – as from a traffic light, they kept their heads upright. I developed a fixation on girls – the younger and more inexperienced they looked, the better I liked them and the closer I followed them, watching their every (head) movement. I started getting some strange looks. Though fascinating, this must stop.

I turned to textbooks on neuro-physiology for an explanation. There are complicated inter-actions between the mechanisms in the brain which sense the position of the body relative to the Earth's gravity and the relative position of the eyes. Thus the young driver, till he or she learns to ignore the instinct, will incline the head on turning a corner, in response to the slight centrifugal force, so that the 'natural' position of the eyes is maintained – in terms of 'gravitational' force – but unnatural in visual terms.

Thus a pilot banking his aircraft in a turn *was* in conformity with nature's requirements. The resultant problem – and the solution – did not occur to me until two closely related incidents happened at about this time.

I was feeling ill enough one day to be confined to bed and, when some food was brought to my bedside, I remained lying down with my head on the pillow and attempted to feed myself in that position. It was quite clear that my co-ordination and judgement of distances were grossly disturbed and I succeeded in spilling liquid on the floor whilst attempting to drink. At first I thought it was due to my fever, but this was disproved when I sat up and had no further trouble.

A simple experiment can demonstrate this. Turn your head through ninety degrees onto its side so that your eyes are at a right-angle to the horizon. Now try to estimate horizontal distances and compare your estimates with those made with the head in the normal position.

A few days after this event I was sitting on a cliff top by the sea looking at the curling breakers far below. Seagulls were soaring to and fro along the cliff, borne up by the powerful wind coming in from the sea. I watched their graceful banked turns, showing their underbellies and the occasional glimpse of a retracted leg. Suddenly I noticed their heads. Though they banked sharply, their heads always remained parallel to the ground! I could hardly wait to get back into the air on a low-level sortie. I began by doing simulated low-level passes on top of stratus (flat) and small cumulus (fluffy) clouds, in case I misjudged distances. I flew up 'valleys', into and out of the cloud edges – it was very exhilarating. Then back to low-level flying, close to the ground, pulling a lot of G at high speeds with the aircraft in steep banking turns. It worked! No need to pull up a hundred feet from the ground to make a turn and so give notice of one's approach to watching radar. It did, however, create a different problem – that of motion sickness – but that is a subject dealt with in Chapter 5.

With the advent of the carrier steam catapult in the early 1950s, another threat to the physiological limits of the human frame was posed – or so the ever-present sceptics suggested. Ignorance is an excellent culture medium for fear, gloom and despondency.

Prior to the development of a British invention, the steam catapult, take-offs from carriers had been a comparatively leisurely affair with the ship steaming into wind and contributing about half the required airspeed to get the aircraft airborne. Increased take-off speeds could be reached by using either the old-fashioned catapult or a series of rockets slung under the wings, termed Rocket Assisted Take-Off Ground (RATOG). Rumours circulating amongst pilots believed that the steam catapult was capable of exerting a force equal to three or even four times the force of gravity in accelerating the aircraft off the ship's bow. Questions were posed as to how this might effect a pilot's ability to fly the aircraft at the moment of becoming airborne. Would he become disorientated? Perhaps his eye balls would become flattened – like a football being kicked, thus putting his instruments as well as the outside world out of focus. It was even suggested that pilots would need to wear 'pebble-lensed' goggles like those worn following an operation for the removal of a cataract, to be discarded as soon as normal flight was attained. Stern stuff indeed – a threat to the very ability of the Royal Navy to operate its next generation of jet aircraft.

Rumours such as this were the very stuff that the medical team at Farnborough thrived on. A healthy non-lethal dose of operational tension kept the Lab in business and was also stimulating for the task of basic research, upon which operational research was so dependent. Moreover, the fears of acceleration-induced-myopia were not totally unfounded in fact, for about this time aircraft with considerably greater powers of acceleration were coming into squadron service, and their pilots *were* having sight problems.

The then revolutionary Canberra (also built as the B57 in America) was a case in point. There were reports of unexplained accidents involving these aircraft, and the circumstances surrounding them were invariably either at night or in conditions of poor visibility. They all followed a similar pattern, with the aircraft abandoning an approach to land at a fairly late stage when its speed was comparatively low. The pilot would either decide to overshoot or be instructed so to do, necessitating the application of a lot of engine power, retracting his undercarriage, followed by the aircraft accelerating away with a rapid build-up of speed – being flown by visual reference to instruments. As the aircraft climbed away, the speed built up and it would follow a trajectory-like flight and dive into the ground, still with full engine power being applied.

It was not long before the reason became apparent and

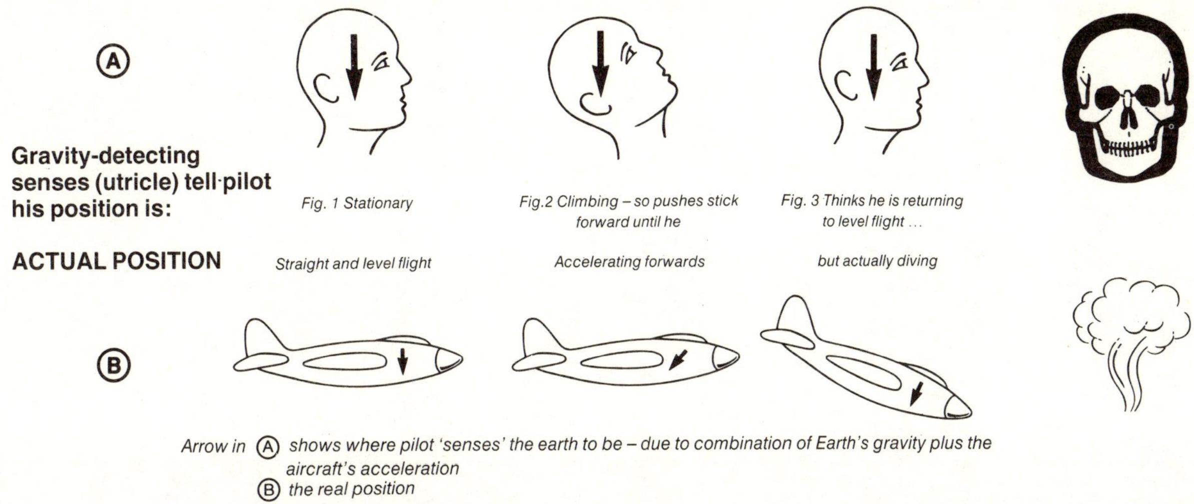

Figure 1 shows how the utricle 'indicates' relative to the eyes – at rest. So long as the eyes have an outside visual reference point, signals from the utricle can be ignored. If the eyes are shut or in darkness, the signals will serve to interpret the angle of tilt of the head.

Figure 2: Should the body (including the head) be accelerated in a forward direction, the utricle will indicate the Earth's gravitational pull as being behind, i.e. it hangs backwards like a plumb-line. This will give the impression, in flying an aircraft, that the aircraft is *climbing*, so …

Figure 3: … corrective action instinctively, should the pilot disbelieve his instruments (which alone will reveal the true position), is to push the control column forward. Being already at a low height, the aircraft dives into the ground before the error is recognized.

The problem is a variant of 'the leans', though the illusion is caused by a different organ in the brain, for illusions of 'turning' are caused by the semi-circular canals (see Chapter 5).

steps were taken to alert pilots flying Canberras as to the dangers. Flying the Lab Canberra on pressure-suit trials confirmed what was happening.

An organ in the brain, called the utricle, 'senses' where the Earth is in relation to the body's position – in the manner of a plumb-line. It sends messages to the brain to take up the position appropriate to being upright and prevents us, under normal conditions, falling over.

It was against this background that the spectre of the steam catapult was brought to the aeronautical physiologists at Farnborough for investigation. After discussing the problem it was felt that the best and safest way to evaluate the project was on the ground. It was fortuitous that, for an entirely different purpose, Colonel John Paul Stapp, a medical officer in the United States Air Force, was conducting high acceleration and deceleration trials in a rocket sledge on a track in a Californian desert. For experimental purposes he was strapped onto a rocket-propelled trolley which was driven along a track, reaching a speed in excess of 600 mph before being dramatically stopped by a series of hydraulic rams, and so imposing very high deceleration forces on Stapp's body. His feat was highly publicized at the time (early 1950s) with full technicolour coverage producing some most spectacular results. Colonel Stapp claimed to be 'the fastest man on earth'. However, the real purpose of his experiment was to see what would happen to the human body when subjected to decelerations produced when an aircraft crashed, and how to protect the human frame by using suitable restraining harness.

It was suggested to the Admiralty that the best way to establish whether there was anything to be feared from the acceleration from the steam catapult was to simulate the acceleration – and more – on a track, as in Colonel Stapp's project, and we studied the Stapp results with keen interest.

It was clear that deceleration forces experienced in

aircraft crashes fell into two categories: first, those associated with the approach and landing phase, or during and immediately following an attempted take-off; second, during mid-flight, such as might happen by flying into a mountain or similar in-flight catastrophe.

In the first case the deceleration impact was below 20G, and Stapp's work showed conclusively that the human frame could be protected against this sort of force, but in the second category there would be near total disintegration of both man and machine, and protection was impracticable.

Our pleas to the authorities for facilities of even modest proportions compared with the Americans' were, in true British fashion, treated with derision. We were told to make use of what facilities were already in existence and to produce tangible results, with recommendations, as soon as possible. The omens were not favourable. However, I found a natural ally in Squadron Leader Fred Latham, who was also interested in carrying out acceleration experiments and was waiting for a human centrifuge to be built at Farnborough. Fred was a qualified navigator as well as having a good medical degree and was useful as a guide around Europe in an aircraft. I never knew him to get lost, and he was rarely at a loss for words either.

We took stock of our assets. There was a half-mile abandoned length of old railway track at Farnborough. It had been used some time earlier for propelling dummies to see what damage they received under various 'crashes' during the early work on ejection seats. The track was constructed from old rusty rails salvaged from the Army railway at Bordon and pronounced 'no longer fit for human use'. We thought that at a pinch this would do for our purposes. We also found a sort of perspex 'stage-coach' which looked not unlike the way the front end of a modern high-speed '125' passenger train might look before painting. We thought this could be fitted with runners so that it would slide like a sledge on the rails. Wheels were out of the question on account of the poor state of the track.

A method of propelling the 'stage-coach' was the next requirement. This proved easier than we dared hope. The Admiralty had made it quite clear that we could expect minimum financial help from them. However, necessity being the mother of invention, we were lucky enough to find a young scientist attached to the RAE who had a healthy interest in explosives. Moreover, he had access to a considerable cache of obsolete – and 'time-expired' for all we knew – rockets (RATOGs, see p. 69) which had been manufactured many years previously to assist aircraft to achieve take-off speed aboard carriers. A scheme was drawn up for lashing these together in banks of four, six, eight, ten and twelve, arranged so they could be fired in succession, thus providing a to-be-hoped-for smooth build-up in acceleration to a theoretical peak of about 14G – to be determined in the light of experience!

We installed a standard aircraft seat on the trolley and, as a rough-and-ready measure of how the 'pilot' performed whilst being 'catapulted', rigged up some simple instrumentation. This consisted of a white circle which was moved by an electric motor at random over a screen and which had to be covered by a cross which was under the control of the pilot when he moved his control column.

The trolley was fired – empty – on a few experimental runs. To make sure it stopped before reaching the end of the track, a standard aircraft arrester gear from an old carrier was installed at the far end, with arrester wires stretched across the 'railway' line. So far so good.

We received a few enquiries from passers-by and local residents as the not-so-muffled explosions grew in intensity and frequency. Since one of our technical helpers had been born in Eire and was proud of his Dublin accent, in our own interests, as well as his, we forbade him to answer any enquiries as to the purpose of the explosions.

The day for the first human test run arrived. The method of firing the rockets was daunting. It had to be done by remote control, and our explosives expert, having made sure we were tightly strapped into the seat, would retreat to a safe hide-out behind some boulders about forty yards away, paying out wire from a reel as he went. Before plugging the wire into a detonator, he would come to the front of the 'carriage', make a sort of grimace meant to convey reassurance and disappear. One knew that the next action would be violent and could be expected in anything from twenty to forty seconds, depending on the dampness of the explosives and the presence of other traffic (it was alongside the main Farnborough runway and one did not wish to startle real flying pilots taking off).

During this pause I realized I was at the 'wrong' end of that notice which reads 'Danger – Quarry Blasting – Keep Clear' when ... whoops, a bang (felt rather than heard – they always *said* you never heard the crack of the rifle that hit you!) and I was off down the railway line, by this time already slowing down with the friction of the sledge on the rails. The contraption stopped. I unstrapped and got out and looked back. A thick haze of cordite was slowly drifting from the start of the track over the top of the nearby hangar where our aircraft were so admirably looked after and serviced by the civilians attached to Structural Mechanical and Engineering (SME) flight, in a deserted corner of Farnborough airfield – an appropriate place, I thought, for the experiment.

We managed to persuade a sympathetic tractor driver who normally towed aircraft around the airfield to pull the trolley back to the start, and we carried out a couple more runs that day to see how they went. At the end of the third run, as I was helping to pull the trolley back, I was met by the foreman of the SME flight, holding a metal disc weighing perhaps a quarter of a pound. He was apologetic but firm.

'I know you doctors are always up to new tricks, usually

in the air, and we always try to look after you and keep your aircraft safe with your various ideas, but I've had a complaint from one of my fitters. He was nearly hit by this metal disc when you startled the living daylights out of us with a noise fit to raise the dead; the building shook and two of these came through the window.'

It was the only time these splendid men who looked after us protested at our work, and they certainly put up with a lot. However, honour was satisfied by building a fine mesh metal guard around the departing 'terminus' of our railway, and the rides continued with increasing ferocity.

Because of the age of the rockets, occasionally one of them in the 'bank' would not ignite, resulting in a much lower thrust or even no thrust at all if the detonator failed. I well recall acknowledging the encouraging grimace of the explosives enthusiast, prior to his thirty-second dash across rough ground to take cover behind boulders, but suddenly I perceived my explosives friend appear in my peripheral field of vision, wave his hands – and disappear. Now what? Was he saying 'It's all abandoned'? Even as I relaxed, I wondered if he was just letting me know of some delay and I'd be off in a minute. I tensed up again – ready for anything. Perhaps he'd doubled the charge and being unsafe to unload he was going to let me have the full benefit! I closed my eyes till a babble of voices came near and I realized the trolley door was opening. I then learned that it had been discovered that the arrester wire at the far end of the track and been disconnected and my colleagues had assumed that I would prefer not to ride that day!

Eventually we got most of the 'bugs' out of the system and got a regular programme under way, but the unsophisticated method of getting the sledge away remained as before. Not for us the nice firm count-down of Cape Kennedy: 'Five … four … three … two … we have ignition … one … lift off!' Just the ever-uncertain wait and then … bang!

When the rockets became more reliable, we called for volunteers. The Lab was never short of candidates for the various medical experiments; the Empire Test Pilot School students based at Farnborough at that time were always enthusiastic and excellent subjects. We worked the trolley progressively up to a maximum acceleration of about 12G, which propelled it forwards from a standstill to about 60 mph in about 1½ seconds, which could still show up well in a modern *Autocar Road Test Report* – if performance were to be the criterion. Comfort and ride did not, however, match the performance!

We prepared a carefully calibrated series of experiments, collating subjects' performances against increasing accelerations. The subjects were drawn from a wide sample, ranging from experienced test pilots to some with little or no flying experience. The results were reassuring, and we were able to convince their lordships that no visual or disorientation disturbance would be encountered on the new steam catapult. It has since been confirmed under operational conditions experienced by all the Western Powers' navies.

The Farnborough rocket railway had justified its existence, despite any slight inconvenience caused by irregular time-keeping.

There was one casualty, however. Some of the earlier rockets would have failed to meet the Trades Description Act and gave a performance which could only be described as less than satisfactory in terms of smoothness of ride. Some years later my friends would chaff me because I was unable to drink my beer without spilling a considerable amount, such was my 'shake' on raising my glass. Giving injections became an embarrassment, and patients gave me the sort of look which would have encouraged older doctors to retire. An X-ray revealed the cause – I had broken my neck.

5 *The Eyes Have It*

One of the functions of the medical flying section was to discuss physiological ideas with other doctors at the Lab and put them to the test in the air. In doing so, the non-pilot physiologists suffered considerable discomfort, even personal risk, to prove their point, as they were always anxious to participate personally in all airborne experiments whenever possible.

Wing Commander Tom Whiteside was particularly interested in the cause, effect and prevention of motion sickness. I was never certain as to how much his own personal susceptibility to this affliction played a part in his interest. His enthusiasm certainly extended to the designing of a portable 'receptacle' for the returned stomach contents and putting it to effective use in the Lab aircraft.

Tom charted what he termed the 'vomit threshold', which was when the complete stomach contents had been disgorged into this portable receptacle. On those days when he was 'experimenting', he would take care to have a good breakfast, and I do believe he counted the eggs on their being regurgitated. 'I counted them in and I counted them all back.' He would also draw up a flight pattern to be followed (as often as not in cloud) made up of a series of gyrations of increasing complexity till his 'vomit threshold' was reached, the whole being timed with a stop-watch (to record 'time to v.t.').

At the time we were using a Mosquito aircraft for early work on the prototype pressure suits, and it was possible to dovetail the two programmes together. For some reason I was, more often than not, invited to make Tom sick – a strange and even perverse requirement, when it is understood to be very poor flying for a pilot to return a passenger to the ground pale, much less minus his stomach contents! In the Mosquito the passenger, Tom, sat alongside the pilot, me, so we would go, climb into cloud and then, monitored by Farnborough under the watchful eyes of their radar, commence increasingly complex sick-making gyrations. Eventually the cramped Mosquito cabin became filled with the unmistakeable odour of undigested breakfast which inevitably preceded Tom's gastric orgasm and he would survey me with balefully reproachful eyes, indicating we could emerge from cloud and prepare to land. For my part, after dozens of such flights, I began to question whether I was a sadist, especially as Tom was always so grateful! We had another affinity – we were born on the same day in 1921.

Another doctor with whom I worked closely was Geoffrey Melville-Jones, who was particularly interested in visual aspects of flying, as was Tom Whiteside. Though not a qualified pilot at that time, Geoffrey later gained his wings and eventually was given the first Chair in Aviation Medicine at McGill University, Montreal. He was recently elected a Fellow of the Royal Society for his work.

I said at the beginning of this story that I would attempt to write in non-technical terms, but to understand how the eyes function a brief explanation is essential. Eyes can be used not only for looking but also to be looked at, for they can give as much information about their owner as a lighthouse does to ships or radio beams to aircraft – the message might be 'Keep your distance' or 'Come closer'.

For our purpose, however, we will confine ourselves to the relationship of the eyes to other important sense organs. First the balancing, gravity-sensing mechanism

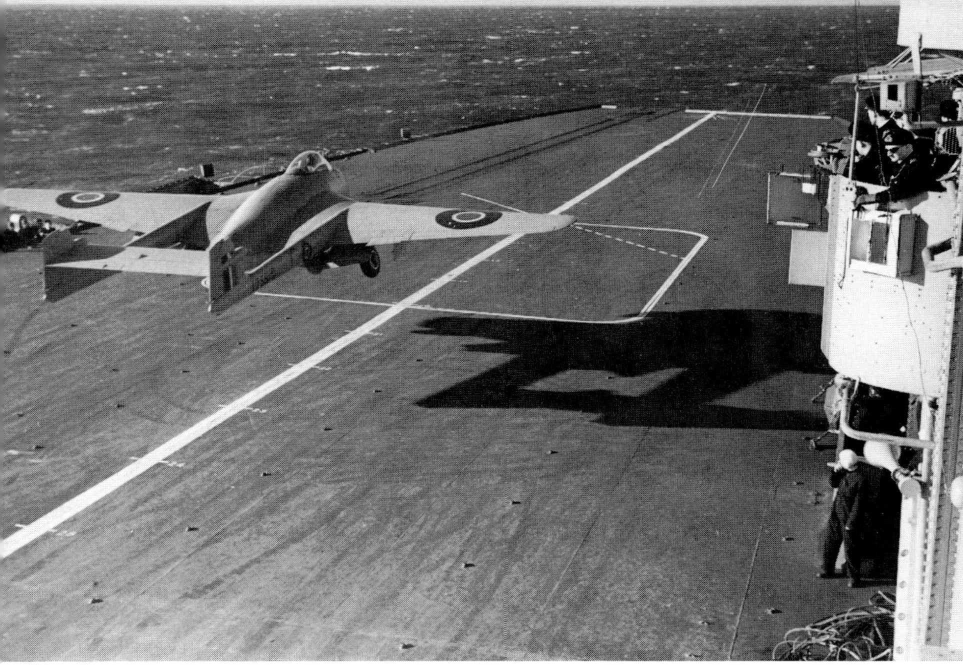

History this day was made. The first jet deck landing by Lt. Cdr. 'Winkle' Brown in a Vampire aboard HMS *Ocean* (1 December 1945)

Firefly Mk V – a comfortable way to arrive aboard a carrier

Hooked but not landed – a Seafire that got away

'Can't you stop? Must you go?' – The author indoctrinating Wing Commander Ruffell Smith into the delights of deck landing with the 'lab's' Meteor 7, No. 619. He is believed to be the oldest pilot to have done a deck landing aboard a carrier

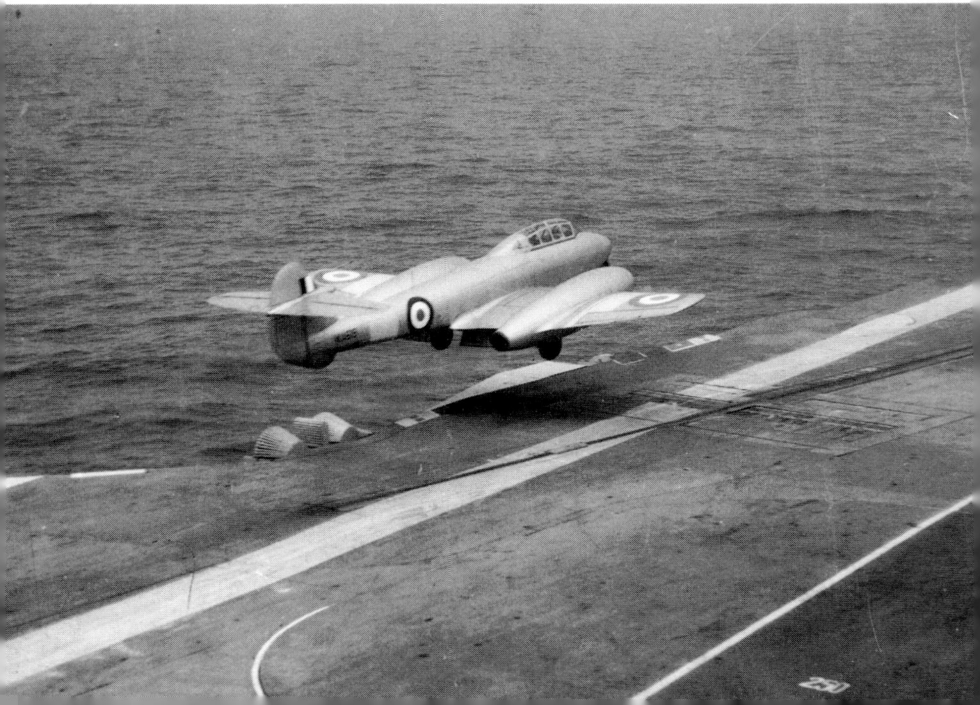

known as the utricle, which acts in the nature of a plumb-line, indicating the position of the earth's gravitational field relative to the body's position. This gives a false indication in relation to the earth's gravity if the body is accelerating or decelerating (see page 71).

The other most important sensing mechanisms are the semi-circular canals, of which there are two sets, situated in the vicinity of each inner ear. They are called semi-circular canals because each set consists of three tubes rather like the inner tube of a bicycle tyre with a small segment cut out. The three tubes are set nearly, but not quite, at right-angles to each other in three different planes. The three missing segments are joined together and sealed by a small chamber, and the whole is filled with fluid. Projecting from the inside of the walls of these tubes into the fluid are minute hairs which can detect any change in movement of the fluid caused by the body turning or twisting. The combination of all the hair receptors' movements are computed by the brain, and so a sense of rotation is presented to the conscious mind.

To begin to understand the relationship of the semi-circular canals with the eyes, imagine a bicycle tyre filled with fluid and then laid flat on its side and gradually spun round. To begin with, the fluid will remain still while the tube rotates. Thus any projecting hairs attached to the inner wall will be bent over as they are dragged through the fluid. They are sensitive enough to discern a rotational movement as little as three degrees per second. The effect on the eyes is to induce a condition called nystagmus, when the eyes will drift slowly from one side to the other as though following a slowly moving object, and then flick quickly back, before repeating the cycle, about two or three times a second. It is an attempt to enable the body to remain orientated to the outside world as the body rotates. It can be likened to a ballet dancer pirouetting round, keeping her face towards the audience before turning her head quickly for the next revolution. There is further purpose in the case of the ballet dancer – she is not giddy on stopping her gyrations, which would otherwise happen. You can readily demonstrate this to yourself by standing up, turning round and round for perhaps a quarter of a minute and then suddenly stopping – but make sure somebody is standing by to catch you.

If the body continues to rotate at the same rate for a minute or more, stability is reached. Consider the bicycle wheel again, with the fluid inside the tyre. Eventually, due to the friction of the tyre wall, the fluid inside the tube will start rotating as well, and it will stabilize when the fluid is rotating at the same speed as the rotating wheel. When this happens to the rotating human body, the hair senses in the affected canal will cease to detect any rotation; the eye nystagmus will cease and all sense of body rotation will cease, except the outside world will appear as a blur as *it* (apparently) rotates. If the rotation stops suddenly, the semi-circular canals remain stationary but the fluid continues moving, sending the delicate hairs in the opposite direction; the eyes will now flick, nystagmus will occur in the reverse direction (observe it for yourself on a volunteer) and the now dizzy subject will fall to the ground unless caught.

The stomach acts as a safety valve when the body is beset by unaccounted movements. When the brain receives confusing signals which are at variance with reality – as seen, for example, by the eyes, it has a 'nervous breakdown' which will manifest itself in a variety of ways: first as a warning by the skin becoming moist, followed by emptying the stomach by vomiting – rather like an aircraft jettisoning unwanted fuel to prepare for a crisis.

Malfunctions of the semi-circular canals, due to disease, can be most disabling and one known as Menière's Disease. The sufferer has the greatest difficulty in walking upright, due to giddiness, and any movement can lead to vomiting.

If eye nystagmus in a horizonal plane is induced by

horizontal rotation, it is a short step to demonstrate that the same effect happens in a pitching plane – when the eyes can be made to flick up and down (vertical nystagmus). What would be the effect of rotating the body in the rolling plane? The answer was not long in coming.

About this time (1954) power-assisted controls were making possible very high rates of roll in aircraft. Peter Twiss, the test pilot for Fairey Aviation, was reporting some interesting effects following the very high rate of roll achieved in the experimental Fairey Delta aircraft. Geoffrey Melville-Jones, who was studying how eyes were used during flight, and I did a lot of flying together. He was a quiet, thoughtful and considerate person with whom it was a great joy to work, and we spent many happy and fruitful hours in aircraft together. He plotted the Fairey machine's rate of roll in relation to control movement and, by superimposing nerve impulse and time for decision-taking initiations, was able to demonstrate, quite conclusively, that a pilot flying reversing rolls, i.e. two or three to the left, followed by a similar number to the right etc, would have to initiate (in his brain) the roll to the right before the preceding roll to the left had actually been commenced.

About this time I became interested in how pilots utilized their eyes during an approach to a carrier deck. An experiment was devised to provide the answer, by photographing pilots' eyes during the critical approach and landing phase, in a variety of jet aircraft. One of the aircraft we used was the Meteor 7, a dual controlled twin-engined jet used for training.

The pilot to be photographed would fly the aircraft from the front seat with a second pilot in the rear seat. A camera was mounted just behind the front pilot's shoulder, and a mirror was fixed in front of his face. This enabled close-up pictures to be taken of his eyes, which could later be analysed frame by frame in the laboratory. Thus a complete record was made of how a pilot used his eyes during each experimental landing. The proportion of the time spent looking at the runway and instruments, and the frequency and duration of each glance, was recorded. Even how often he blinked was noted. (The application of these researches are described in Chapter 8.)

Using the technique of photographing pilots' eyes enabled Geoffrey to demonstrate a hitherto unknown eye movement. The phenomenon of lateral nystagmus (side-to-side 'flicking') of the eyes during rotation was well known; it was also easy to demonstrate that vertical nystagmus would occur, by doing a series of continuing 'loops' in the aircraft; when the remaining (rotational) plane was studied, the pilot carrying out a series of rapid rolls, the resulting ciné pictures showed with great clarity that the eyeball also twisted in its socket in a rotational nystagmus movement – quickly 'rotating' in one direction and then slowly untwisting in another direction.

I have gone into some physiological detail because this story has a wider interest and can be demonstrated by anyone on a commercial flight.

One last technical fact has to be explained. The minute sensing hairs projecting into the endolymph fluid contained in the semi-circular canals are sensitive enough to detect a change in the fluid's movement, resulting from the body rotating at a minimum rate of three degrees per second (technically accelerating at three degrees per second per second). By coincidence this is the same rate of rotation as an aeroplane altering course in a Rate 1 turn. This is a standard rate of turn used by commercial flights and will not usually be noticed by passengers. However, to achieve this rate of turn, the modern jet aircraft has to bank quite steeply when commencing such a turn. The rate of application of the turn, i.e. in a rotational plane, is usually quite significant – high enough to stimulate the appropriate semi-circular canals. The result is that the eyes 'rotate'. During such rotation, if the passenger looks ahead at a convenient bulkhead, *it* will appear to rotate – though, of course, relative to the passenger, it has not moved.

Thus, without knowing the reason, a passenger is aware when his aircraft starts to turn. But, I hear you say, of course you are aware when an aircraft alters course, even in cloud or at night, and of course you are right – but for the wrong reason in that the semi-circular canals have signalled the turn, making the visual 'turn' appear natural.

6 *Gliding, Belly-Flopping and the Big Dipper*

To fly with Johnny Howitt, a medical doctor pilot who retired as a Group Captain, was to be compared to visiting the London Palladium with the Crazy Gang in full cry. Whatever the situation, Johnny turned it to humour. It was rumoured that he was given his well-deserved Air Force Cross 'for services to the world of aeronautical entertainment'. Behind all the clowning, though, Johnny was one of the most competent pilots ever to take to the air.

On one of his flights, due to a combination of factors outside his control, Johnny was diverted to Farnborough whilst flying a Meteor. He knew he was desperately short of fuel, so he was allowed to join the circuit on the downwind leg, with plenty of spare height in case he ran out of fuel, which he did. The circuit had been cleared to allow him to make an unobstructed approach to land. His clearly anguished voice was heard in Air Traffic Control announcing that his port engine had stopped, followed by muttering something about 'Never did like one-engined landings – bloody dangerous, liable to turn upside down and other lethal habits.' Air Traffic watched his continuing progress on the downwind leg, and commencing his final turn towards the runway, undercarriage coming down, a little flap, all in accord with a textbook single-engined approach, a high rate of descent, with the remaining jet issuing a subdued whine. Then suddenly Johnnie's voice, clearly relieved, announced: 'Remaining engine stopped. No fuel left, so now no risk of fire in the event of miscalculation landing.' Then, as an afterthought, as he neared his perfect touchdown: 'Always did want to take up gliding.'

Not such a happy experience was enjoyed by Conrad Bazarnik in a similar aeroplane some time later. Conrad was a Polish-born doctor pilot attached to the Institute of Aviation Medicine. His not inconsiderable Polish charm was a useful asset in achieving our objectives on foreign trips.

Conrad was carrying out an air test after the Meteor 7 had undergone a major overhaul, and was carrying as his observer in the rear seat Dr Tony Gurney. Ironically they intended to combine the air test with an experiment in communications between front and rear cockpits. Unbeknown to Conrad, the latches holding the folding canopy in place had not been properly aligned and, at 350 knots, with a loud bang, the whole canopy parted from the aircraft, leaving Tony Gurney semi-conscious with a large, bleeding gash on his scalp. The flight ceased to be enjoyable; flying in an open cockpit at that speed is an experience best avoided. Conrad had no reason to disbelieve that his bleeding passenger was a corpse. No communication was possible, for both helmets had been torn off in the blast, so Conrad had no option but to make straight for Farnborough in his crippled aircraft, carrying a full fuel load.

He came straight in, hoping that Air Traffic had spotted his plight – fortunately they had. The plane came in faster than would be normal to allow for the higher stalling speed, but not fast enough, for the loss of the canopy had increased the speed at which the aircraft stalled by more than 20 knots. It stalled well above the runway at a high speed and dropped like a stone onto its belly undercarriage, collapsing and skidding along on the fuel tanks, catching fire as it went. Eventually it stopped and Conrad and the 'corpse' in the back left the blazing scene as quickly as they could, sustaining burns but miraculously without serious injury.

Mayhem broke out, and Conrad was quite unjustly reprimanded. Later, however, this reprimand was quashed and changed to an award of the AFC. The aircraft was a write-off but steps were taken to ensure that a similar accident could never be repeated by introducing an extra pre-flight check to confirm the alignment of the canopy handles. This was one of the very rare accidents involving a Lab aircraft in many years of experimental flying.

After I had been at Farnborough for nearly two years it was becoming evident that the Naval Medical Department was becoming increasingly restive about my remaining much longer. Tradition and force of habit seemed to compel the Naval Medical Department to 'shake the bag' and call 'All change!' every two years. To their eyes, I, as a junior medical officer, appeared to be recalcitrant, which I was. There was a series of very interesting prototype aircraft beginning to fly at that time in the hands of test pilots such as Neville Duke, Bill Bedford, Mike Lithgow, John Derry and a score of others, many of whom were to lose their lives as they probed the then rapidly expanding parameter of aeronautics, and I was loath to leave the Lab in the midst of such fascinating work.

The Naval Medical Department did not feel it quite 'proper' that one of their kind should not be immediately available to do a stint at sea in one of the great ships of the line (Britain still had HMS *Vanguard* in commission at that time) and continue the noble tradition of walking the quarter-deck under the shadow of sixteen-inch guns. I had no alternative but to play 'politics' if I was to stay at Farnborough long enough to make a contribution to naval flying. The Medical Department, however, was not altogether too pleased when it came to their notice that I was beginning to win friends in other departments at the Admiralty – the Departments of Air Warfare and Training. These departments were becoming increasingly interested in the research work being carried out at Farnborough, and in this connection my official title of Naval Medical Liaison Officer was useful to bridge the gap and smooth the rivalry that periodically burst out between the Navy and the Air Force. I was mindful that I had to play the role of politician and was ably instructed and much helped in this skill by Air Commodore W.K. Stewart, the commanding officer at that time of the Institute of Aviation Medicine.

Bill Stewart had carried out a lot of the original work on oxygen equipment and, along with Air Commodore Harry Roxburgh, Group Captain Tony Barwood and others, had already made a considerable contribution to physiological aviation equipment. Perhaps Bill's major contribution was the result of extensive trials on ejection-seat accelerations and their effect on the human body. His findings made possible the development of the Martin-Baker ejection seat, installed as standard equipment in most military aircraft throughout the western world today.

In spite of his wide experience in aviation, Bill Stewart had never visited a naval ship and certainly had not experienced an 'arrested' landing at sea. Though he was not a qualified pilot, I determined for many reasons to introduce him to shipboard flying, preferably in person. It was my practice during my appointment at Farnborough to visit naval air stations and carriers as frequently as possible, to keep in touch with my 'mother service'. Sly comments were sometimes levelled at my 'salute', implying that it was taking on an RAF slant. Quite untrue of course!

My opportunity came when one day I visited the naval air station at Ford, in Sussex (now an open prison – as one wag commented, 'They never changed it!'). I took the Lab Canberra, which was equipped with some experimental breathing equipment which I thought might be of interest to the naval squadron of Attacker aircraft stationed there. I was also able to give a few demonstration flights to some of the naval pilots, for at that time the Canberra was still a new and novel aircraft and the Navy was still mostly operating piston-engined aircraft. Gus Hathaway, Commanding Officer of a Firefly squadron briefly disembarked from the carrier *Theseus*, was delighted to have a flight in the Canberra. I seized my chance when I heard that he was to embark his squadron aboard *Theseus* in the next few days and that, due to illness, he was short of a pilot. I offered to get his aircraft on board and, still glowing from his trip in the Canberra, he accepted. However, catching sight of my red stripes and, perhaps with a mind to the Geneva Convention, he came back and said that, the aircraft had to carry out live rocket-target practice somewhere on Dartmoor before landing aboard *Theseus*. He was clearly having second thoughts about doctors, who should be confined to their sickbay dispensing pink pills to pale people.

I had an aversion to live ammunition of any sort but was determined to press home my advantage, so I said I would be back at dawn the next day in time for briefing, together with a senior RAF doctor, who wished to experience a deck landing 'as he did not believe it possible'. I saw him waver and wrestle with Service loyalties and the opportunity to let the Air Force see how we operated. I had won my point. He agreed I should come. Bill Stewart was delighted but, like me, had doubts about the rocketry. However, he conceded.

The next day we drove down to Ford before dawn, which, when it came, revealed a high wind, low, scudding cloud and a sea that was made up of more white than grey. At briefing we were told the weather had already cleared from the west, on Dartmoor, but the sea would remain rough and the area where we would rendezvous with the ship would remain subject to squally showers.

The 'rocket' briefing was less to my liking. Being medical, I had avoided this sort of aggressive flying on all possible occasions.

On this sortie, with Bill occupying the navigator's seat, we took off from Ford in poor weather, to be led to the range on Dartmoor by the flight leader. I was to 'formate' on his aircraft, another form of flying I detested, especially as it turned out on this occasion that one was formation-flying in cloud for the most part of the hour-long flight. Not that I disliked cloud – I don't and have always enjoyed all instrument flying, but I prefer to be alone under such conditions.

The weather cleared as forecast by the time we reached Exeter. The briefing had been straightforward. The target on Dartmoor would be marked out by a series of rings, and two aircraft at a time would fly in a circuit at 5,000 feet, taking it in turns to dive down onto the target and fire the rockets.

What follows I recount with some embarrassment, and it is only the passage of time that tempers my humiliation.

After the first run and climbing away, I heard Bill's Glaswegian voice comment that he couldn't see the result ' … but he'd enjoyed the scenery, visibility was good and he could identify Plymouth'. After the last rocket had been fired, the range officer came up on the radio with our results. I blanched behind my oxygen mask as he told me that three of the rockets were 'just within the target area' but the fourth had struck a sheep, 'now believed dead'. I vowed I would never indulge in such violence again but restrict my flying to the activities to which I was more suited.

We formed up into a loose flight of three aircraft and flew low out to sea to make our rendezvous with *Theseus*. We soon found her, turning into wind, heaving in a grey rough sea, the flight deck awash from rain and sea spray. Bill muttered something about its resembling a Dinky toy but this time, compared to the earlier rocket débâcle, I did slightly better and was the first to get aboard, with Bill giving a running commentary from the back seat. He was given a warm welcome in the ante-room and asked how he had enjoyed it. He said, 'It was better than the big dipper' – but he was relieved there was no water-splash!

If there had been a water-splash, and if our plane had sunk, I might well not have lived to tell this tale. The life-saving invention of the underwater ejection seat was the work of John Rawlins, my colleague as a naval doctor at the Lab. But let us start at the beginning …

With Bill Stewart now firmly supporting the cause of the Fleet Air Arm and, by this time, Pat Ruffell Smith giving active support by allowing me access to his aeroplanes, it was encouraging to note that Admiralty departments were at last aware of the medical research that was being conducted at the Institute of Aviation Medicine at Farnborough on physiological equipment essential to naval pilots flying the next generation of naval aircraft being planned – aircraft like the Sea Vixen and Scimitar.

Physiological problems had already caused the Admiralty headaches as a result of the earlier Sea Venoms and other aircraft not being pressurized, making a significant number of experienced and otherwise medically fit pilots unfit to fly because of their susceptibility to 'bends', a condition similar to divers' bends or Caisson disease. (Caused by nitrogen bubbles forming in the body – usually in previously damaged joints or in the central nervous system, it can be very incapacitating, excruciatingly painful, even causing paralysis and sometimes coma and death.) A good deal of my time was therefore taken up acting as an official guide to a succession of senior naval officers who would visit Farnborough from the Admiralty for a conducted tour round the various laboratories, where the thirty RAF medical officers were carrying out a great deal of applied and basic research into aviation medicine and associated areas.

By this time John Rawlins was beginning to identify problems. He was to make a significant contribution to naval pilots' safety, particularly in two specific fields. Eventually he was destined to become the Medical Director General of the Navy at the end of an outstanding career which also saw him ascend in the Order of the British Empire from being a Member to an Officer, and eventually to become a Knight of the Order.

His first contribution was in the study of the dynamics of head injuries. Little progress had been made in this field since Professor Cairns had been instrumental in introducing crash helmets for Army despatch riders during World War II, with a resultant dramatic fall in head injuries. John produced some very convincing figures on blow-absorption, indicating the surprisingly low acceleration forces which could be tolerated by the unprotected skull and how, using the correct energy-absorbing materials, very high-impact blows could be tolerated by a protected head. There was a special need in the Navy for such protection with high-impact forces in the event of an aircraft missing the arrester wires aboard a carrier and entering the 'barrier'. John designed and produced a few prototype helmets (on psychological grounds the words 'crash helmet' was studiously avoided). In due course, as so often happens – as in the nickname 'Mae West' applied to life-jackets, aircrew themselves christened the helmets 'bone domes' and the term stuck.

There then followed a 'publicity' campaign to overcome the initial resistance to the idea of using protective helmets, as has happened with safety belts in cars. Resistance was based on a variety of reasons, each of which had to be overcome with proven facts.

One objection was that, with the increased weight of the bone dome, it would not be possible to keep one's head upright during 'tight turn' manoeuvres. This fear was proved unfounded during airborne trials in the Lab's 'workhorse' aircraft, the Spitfire 22, still used mainly for

G-suit trials. This particular Spitfire was used as, even in the age of jets, it could withstand more G than any other aircraft readily available. Wearing a bone dome, I found I could withstand well over 6G without my head falling over, though I do recall having a sore neck for a few days afterwards. With hindsight it may well have contributed to the cervical spondylitis which afflicts me today. (My mother-in-law also commented – unkindly I thought at the time – that I was developing a neck like a bull!)

Test pilots were the first to show an active interest in wearing bone domes and, with the support of the students at the Empire Test Pilots School, whose mess we used at Farnborough and whose aircraft we borrowed from time to time, John commenced a campaign of measuring skulls, an important step, and tailor-making bone domes for all test pilots requiring helmets.

One such pilot was John Derry, who was test flying with John Wilson the two DH 110 prototypes. Before Derry could collect his helmet, which was waiting in my office, he was tragically killed when the DH 110 broke up at the Farnborough Air Show, catapulting one of the engines into the crowd and killing over thirty spectators. This incident gives me an opportunity to pay tribute to the wives of that gallant band of test pilots in the 1950s, for many were widowed. John Derry's wife witnessed her husband's fatal crash from the pilots' tent on that awesome day. In the stunned silence that followed the crash, she was reported as saying quietly, 'Would somebody give me a cigarette please?'

Shortly afterwards I had the opportunity of flying the remaining DH 110 prototype, which had finished its test-flying programme but still had a few spare flying hours left. Partly for sentimental reasons, I took John Derry's helmet with me – in fact, John and I were the same head size. Thereafter, almost as a concession to superstition, I never made another flight without wearing his bone dome – possibly on the principle that lightning seldom strikes twice. John Derry was a first-class pilot and a very fine man.

The day for my indoctrination to the DH 110 dawned bright and clear, and I ferried myself over to Hatfield, where the aircraft was kept. John Wilson, who had completed most of the developmental flying on the prototype, briefed me. He was somewhat despondent, for the Javelin had just been chosen in preference to the DH 110 to go into production for the RAF. In my view there was no comparison between the two aircraft from a flying standpoint, for the 110 was docile and a delight to fly. Several years later, belatedly, it was put into production for the Royal Navy as the Sea Vixen.

I took off from Hatfield and crossed the south coast at 30,000 feet in a cloudless sky. The sea below was still, like a millpond. I could see a fishing boat with a flock of attendant seagulls awaiting the pickings. I had often wondered how one should aim a sonic boom, suspecting that it was necessary to 'undershoot' to allow for refraction through the Earth's varying atmospheric pressure, in the same way that a stick is optically 'bent' on entering water. I rolled the aircraft over and put it into a forty-five degree dive, aiming the nose at a point on the sea surface about fifteen degrees short of the fishing boat. I watched the Mach meter increase from 0.7 to 1.05 Mach before gently pulling back. As I eased the throttles and flew low alongside the fishermen, they waved and clapped their hands over their ears – it had worked.

Shortly afterwards the Admiralty gave approval for all naval pilots to be equipped with bone domes, a decision quickly followed by the Air Ministry.

Until now it had been the procedure for pilots escaping from doomed aircraft to open their canopies and climb out. After the introduction of the ejection seat it was still necessary to get rid of the canopy before ejection, either by opening it or, later, by means of a small explosive charge which blew it clear. Seconds are precious in the final

Going, going, gone – Scimitars are launched from HMS *Ark Royal* at anchor in Grand Harbour, Malta, by courtesy of the steam catapult

A classic arrival of a Scimitar – note the nose up attitude denoting the correct speed to pick up an arrester wire

HMS *Bulwark* at speed launching her Sea Hawk fighters

HMS *Ark Royal* launches a Sea Vixen – note the strop falling away

moments of a doomed aircraft, but with the advent of the bone dome it was first suspected, and then supported by practical tests, that it would be possible, and essentially quicker, for the pilot to eject himself through the canopy. This became standard ejection procedure.

The decision to issue bone domes to all aircrew in the two Services presented a 'sizing' problem of some magnitude. To this end the project was handed over to Dr Geoffrey Morant, an anthropologist at the Lab, inveterate pipe-smoker, capable of assessing bodily statistics more accurately than a fashion designer. Geoffrey was unassuming, retiring and co-operative – but only so long as he had his pipe in his hand. The suggestion that it would be helpful if he could accompany us visiting Navy and Air Force Squadrons produced a guarded acquiescence – only on condition that his pipe came too and that, like the flame at the Arc de Triomphe, it should never be extinguished. This posed a problem, for it was clear that Geoffrey might opt to travel by train if his protective smoke screen were to be removed. It was clearly impractical to transport him in the Canberra, even though one misguided researcher offered an oxygen mask to accommodate a pipe. Eventually Geoffrey agreed to travel in the station Viking – *and* to obey the 'No Smoking' signs. Thus we turned for a time into a 'charter' flight, much to the astonishment of naval personnel when this airliner would arrive and disgorge a wholly medical crew plus Geoffrey.

After collating the sizes and shapes of the aircrew, the bone domes were manufactured. John Rawlins supervised their issue, and he and I visited all naval air stations to answer questions on their use.

After one such visit John and I were returning to Farnborough from Lossiemouth, in the north of Scotland. Our take-off had been delayed till after sunset, and we were witness, over the radio, to a most dramatic incident. We were flying a Balliol two-seater aircraft, and the night was clear and calm. The trip from Losssiemouth was calculated to take about 2½ hours, and the forecast was for fog developing over East Anglia later in the night. The month was late November and, after a particularly busy day in our capacity as 'hatters', we took off from Lossiemouth just as the sun was setting, in a cloudless sky. Though not a qualified pilot, John, like most of the doctors at Farnborough, was an excellent man to have as a co-pilot, and as it got dark he took his turn at flying the aircraft south. 'Fairy lights' glittering from Scottish villages gave way to vast illuminated displays of the cities, Edinburgh, Tyneside – and then ceased. We had reached the fog.

We were listening to various radio messages, and it was clear that night-flying aircraft in East Anglia were being recalled owing to the unexpectedly early formation of fog over their bases. By this time we could just hear Farnborough calling us, and we obtained a fix confirming that our course was OK and that their cloud base was about 1,000 feet, which was keeping the fog at bay. There did not seem to be any need to consider a possible diversion at this stage, so John and I passed the next forty minutes listening to the drama taking place around a particular RAF base in East Anglia which had some six Hunter aircraft airborne, so far as we could gather. The fog that had formed so unexpectedly quickly was thick and, with no alternative base open nearby, the air traffic controller was doing his utmost to guide his pilots back to base. He managed to talk four aircraft down but dwindling fuel, after several abortive attempts to land, left no alternative but to instruct the remaining two aircraft to climb up to a few thousand feet, set them on a course which would take them out to sea and order the pilots to eject. As the second pilot to eject made his last transmission, 'Aircraft trimmed straight and level, course 090 degrees, speed 160 knots – ejecting', followed by an eerie silence, we felt very lonely in the blackness, until the familiar and friendly, confident voice of Bill Pendrey at Farnborough called us, announcing he had us on his screen and that we should turn forty degrees to port (for identification). Then he took us over till we informed Farnborough we had the runway lead-in lights 400 yards ahead. Another routine day was over.

John Rawlins' other important contribution to aviation came, ironically, from his interest in underwater physiology and diving. Following his successful development of the bone dome and applying it to ejecting through the cockpit canopy, a most unfortunate fatality at sea gave urgency to another application of the ejection seat, which was to occupy most of John's remaining days at Farnborough.

A very capable pilot, Des Russell, was doing deck-landing trials in a Scimitar aboard HMS *Victorious*. Through no fault of his, after a perfect touch-down and engaging an arrester wire with his hook, the aircraft was not fully arrested after pulling the wire to its full extent, and the hook was pulled out of the aircraft before it had come to a halt. Unable to stop on its brakes, the aircraft continued rolling forwards and toppled over the bows into the sea. Des survived this part of the crash, for the aircraft remained on the surface for a short while. As it drifted past the port side of the ship, Des was seen attempting to open his canopy before the aircraft sank. However, it was to no avail, and he lost his life.

Following this tragic event John set out to explore the possibility of a pilot's using an ejection seat in the 'normal' manner from under water. After exhaustive tests he became the first man to use an ejection seat submerged – under controlled conditions, using the Admiralty tank at Loch Fruin. As the tank had glass on one side for observation purposes, his main worry was that the explosive force of the ejection charge might fracture the glass – leaving him high and dry. In the event, it didn't.

7 *Jumping and Batting*

By 1953 we were receiving a steady stream of visitors from the Admiralty. Even the medical department was acknowledging, as other Admiralty departments had already, albeit reluctantly, that aviation medical research was something to be taken seriously and that Farnborough was not just another appointment to be filled every two years on a rotational basis. We were getting a lot of support, including a memorable visit from Admiral Sir Caspar John, a pioneer naval pilot who later became First Sea Lord. He drove himself to Farnborough in an old London taxi – not in uniform, I noted. Captain (later Vice-Admiral) Dick Janvrin, from the Department of Air Warfare, and many others, some to be mentioned later, also descended on us.

It would be unjust if the impression were given that the Royal Air Force had a monopoly of aviation medical research, for there was the equivalent of the RAF Institute of Aviation Medicine in the Naval Air Medical School, which began its days at Eastleigh in Hampshire and in true naval tradition developed peripatetic habits, moving first to Gosport (where Gosport tubes were evolved – a sort of extended stethoscope, to enable an instructor to talk to his pupil) before reaching its final berth at the home of naval aviation, Lee-on-Solent.

The nature of the work that was carried out by this establishment was directed mainly towards the needs of aircrew flying in extended sorties from aircraft-carriers, or at least largely over the ocean. Some of the more problematical areas requiring research in these fields included: how to urinate during a five-hour flight without getting wet (you don't); how to keep dry when you fall in the sea (you don't); how to survive when cast adrift in a dinghy by drinking seawater (you don't).

Perhaps the most potentially interesting project which was put to the medical researchers was how to restore circulation (and life itself) to an aviator who had been forced down in icy waters (Russian convoys were in vogue at the time). Various suggestions were put forward, including brandy, hot water bottles and radiant heat lamps. All were tried with great enthusiasm, till one newly enlisted young doctor suggested putting the frozen subject to bed with an active female and sought authority to conduct the appropriate experiments (no! under no circumstances). History does not relate how, subsequently, good results came to be reported from this theory.

It would be wrong to assume that 'negative' was the watchword for the Naval Air Medical School. It does help this story, however.

One of the earliest medical officers in charge of these experiments at the Air Medical School was Surgeon Captain Boyd Martin, who became well practised at the 'no' regime. At that time Boyd had qualified as a pilot but no medical officer had actually landed an aircraft aboard a carrier, and Boyd was prevailed upon, somewhat reluctantly, to 'volunteer' for the experience. Arrangements were made to strap him into the pilot's seat of a Swordfish (an appropriately gentle aircraft, for Boyd was achieving the figure, and had already developed a personality, akin to that of Robert Morley) and point him and his mount in the direction of HMS *Argus* (an ex-Italian liner) awaiting him just off shore. He arrived safely aboard, making him the first naval surgeon to pilot himself aboard a carrier, but when he was helped from his aircraft and asked whether he would like to perform an encore, his research training came to the rescue and, drawing himself fully upright as he dusted himself down, he said very firmly, 'No, I've got a prescription to be made up at the bar' and he never flew again as a pilot.

As the years passed by, Boyd's resemblance to Robert Morley became even more pronounced. He was always dignified, and this dignity was enhanced by his taking to driving an old Rolls-Royce ('They are so reliable, old boy'). One day whilst he was extolling the qualities of his Rolls, another officer was heard to question the infallibility of the car and, if it was so immune to breakdown, why then the necessity for a starting handle. Boyd was equal to the moment and, fixing the man with an air of a Professor of Medicine, reminded him that no doubt he had a pair of nipples but trusted that he would never be a wet nurse.

Eventually the problem of restoring circulation was solved. The Naval Air Medical School developed the immersion suit – a cumbersome, thick, two-piece garment made of gabardine rubber, with Wellington boots permanently attached. (The Navy, expecting its officers to be all-rounders, presumably fitted the Wellingtons to enable the pilot, having survived, to wade ashore and continue to find his way home on foot.)

A problem which had exercised a succession of medical officers doing their statutory two-year appointment at the school was how to enable the pilot or observer to urinate, once installed in the suit. I suspect the solution emanated from a study of urinating male elephants at the London Zoo.

Naturalists will understand if I explain that the immersion suit was equipped with a rolled rubber tube, some four inches in diameter, coyly hidden beneath a flap in the crutch of the garment. The procedure for urinating was to unfurl the tube to its full flaccid length of fifteen inches or so (like an elephant's penis) and urinate through a hole in the cockpit floor. In spite of the tube's considerable size, it really was a drop in the ocean.

I am a firm believer that much research is self-perpetuating, so I would not be in the least surprised if, even today, some lone researcher at the School is still struggling with this very same problem but, generally speaking, by the mid-50s the role of the Naval Air Medical School was primarily one of training and indoctrination – leaving the bulk of the research to be carried out at Farnborough.

One problem with the immersion suit was that, being voluminous and heavy, it was not unlike a maritime equivalent of a modern space garment, and when donned, it contained a considerable volume of air, giving an impression of a Michelin man with a slow puncture. The effect of this was that, when we did sea trials wearing the garment, the subject would jump into the sea and, until he inflated his life jacket, float helplessly on his back like an overturned Thames barge, his legs clear of the water and threshing the air, like a turtle on its back.

Various suggestions were made, akin to the modern 'vacuum-packed' technique and sucking all surplus air out of the suit after donning it. This would have produced more problems than it solved, some unmentionable, though it might have advanced the fashion of jeans by several years.

A suggestion which held far greater appeal to me, because of the practical work involved, was that the life-jacket which was worn over the immersion suit should be adapted to inflate before dropping into the sea. What, I suggested mischievously, about the pilot who might abandon his aircraft in mid-flight and descended into the sea by parachute? Could the life-jacket be inflated whilst he was still descending in his parachute harness? I had long wanted to do some parachuting, and now I saw my chance. The question could be resolved only by trying it in practice, with a suitably modified life-jacket, and jumping out of an aeroplane appropriately clad in the immersion suit.

Using the ploy I had learned from Pat Ruffell Smith, an appropriately worded memo was soon despatched to the Admiralty, and approval was soon forthcoming for me to go on a parachute-jumping course at RAF Abingdon, where I was ably instructed by Wing Commander Jimmy Blyth, who had done so many jumps that he thought no more about stepping out of an aeroplane than most of us do about stepping into a lift. The course completed, I was then hoist with my own petard. My friends in the Admiralty, picking up my point about the buoyancy of the suit due to trapped air, suggested that the trials should be conducted in a hot climate in a sea of high saline content, thus exacerbating the problem.

Events developed fast, and it was not long before I found myself a member of a small team flying in an RAF Hastings transport aircraft bound for the Bitter Lakes in Egypt in one of the hottest months of the year, clad in a garment specifically designed to be worn inside the Arctic Circle, soon to be despatched from the aircraft into a tepid sea with a buoyancy to match that of the Dead Sea.

Fortunately the trials proved the point. We found that we were able to inflate our life-jackets during our descent, the air bags pushing their way from under the parachute rigging harness, and we barely entered the water at all, not even wetting our faces, floating, right way up, high out of the water. All that remained was to paddle our way ashore, very much as though we were in a canoe.

The modified life-jacket became standard equipment for all aircrew.

Morale of Naval Medical Aircrew received a boost in the early 1950s in the rotund shape of Surgeon Commander (later Surgeon Commodore) Baskerville ('Bask'), who, together with Surgeon Lieutenant Donald McNutt, qualified as a naval observer and wore the appropriate 'wings'. Donald proved a most able navigator in whom I always felt complete confidence. Bask made up for his more advanced years (he was over forty when he gained his observer's wings) by introducing humour to every situation, no matter how critical. He might have been Bud Abbott's twin to look at him. He suffered from 'blocked' ears, so was in constant pain when descending from altitude.

One day he asked if I would fly him down to the naval air station at Culdrose, near Helston, in Cornwall, and practise his navigation on the way. We took off from Farnborough in an old Firefly which was slow enough to give Bask time to work out his navigational problems as we proceeded. The weather, as is so often the case on the south-west peninsula of England, was not promising, with low cloud from Exeter onward. I had a glimpse of Dartmoor through a gap in the clouds when our radio packed up, so I decided to turn south and asked Bask to confirm when we were well out to sea so we could make our descent through the cloud. Having glimpsed Plymouth Hoe through another momentary gap, I was satisfied as to our whereabouts but let Bask continue to worry!

As we descended, Bask got increasing pain from his ears, and several times we had to check our descent in an effort to clear them – but to little avail. Eventually we broke cloud very nearly at sea-level, but to my consternation the Eddystone Light was about fifty yards to our left and *above* us! Much relieved, I made for Falmouth at sea-level, flew up the Helford river and landed at Culdrose, where flying had been suspended for the day due to poor weather. I was glad to land, only to be greeted tartly by Commander (Air) asking what the Hell we thought we were doing and, observing Bask's apparent total deafness due to his ears, ' … and what's more bringing Dr Neptune with you, who is deaf into the bargain!'

Back at Farnborough, I had not lost sight of the original purpose of my being trained to fly – the appallingly high deck-landing accident rate. We had gained the support and confidence of the Admiralty and, having watched thousands of deck landings and done a few myself, I was convinced that the fault lay in human error and probably a breakdown in communication between the pilot and the ship's batsman (Deck Landing Control Officer – DLCO), an experienced pilot who would give guiding signals to pilots on their final approach using a pair of bats. Standing near the stern of the carrier and to one side of the flight deck, he assisted pilots to be at the correct height, speed and position from which to make a safe landing. I applied to go on a DLCO's course.

I had studied many batsmen but will mention five in particular, with very differing styles, to make my point.

Robert Everett, known as R.N. Everett RN, had a flair for the theatrical and, with his delightfully flamboyant manner which should have entitled him to be a paid-up member of Equity, would give a ballet-dance style of performance which was a picture to watch. As the approaching aircraft turned into its final approach towards the flight deck, Bob would emerge from the 'wings' (the batsman's platform) and commence a pirouette across the stage (flight deck), beckoning with his bats, 'willing' the pilot onto the deck as though creating an invisible bond between them. Onlookers new to the game would fear for Bob's safety with the aircraft approaching, as he would prance around, by this time almost in the middle of the flight deck. He appeared as unconcerned for his own safety as a geriatric stalking across a pedestrian crossing with raised umbrella at the height of London's rush hour. The act would finish as the aircraft touched down and Bob gave a theatrical flourish with his bats folded across his chest in the form of a self bear-hug, bending double as the aircraft wings passed over his head, indicating the pilot was now 'home'. The only thing missing was the ballet music.

The second batsman I watched was very much the

professional – a man called Donald McQueen. He made well over a thousand deck landings, a number exceeded only by 'Winkle' Brown (see *Guinness Book of Records*), who for many years whilst at Farnborough was known as the Navy's Chief Test Pilot. Donald's total landings were all without accident, and he was awarded a well-deserved MBE for his careful flying. His 'batting' was like a computer – similar to the professionalism found in modern-day commercial airline pilots. I watched him and noticed that his precise signals were obeyed meticulously in the first few landings by even the most experienced pilots. Gradually, however, pilots would develop their own technique and style which suited them best – perhaps according to their view of the flight deck, and the 'computerized' signal from the Deck Landing Control Officer, however apt it might be, was taken less and less notice of. Thus one could invariably recognize individual pilots on their approach to land by each one's distinctive style.

The third batsman, Stanley Borthwick, a genial Scotsman, whom I was fortunate enough to have for my own initial deck landings, aimed to dominate and even 'possess' the pilot during his landing. I feel sure Stanley would have made a splendid model for an advertising agent in the David Ogilvy tradition, for he always smoked a Sherlock Holmes-style pipe whilst standing on the batting platform practising his art. He would emit smoke whose volume would accurately reflect his satisfaction or otherwise with his pupil. He was an excellent tutor but perhaps prone to personality clashes with experienced pilots who would follow their own inclinations; he was a sincere man.

The last two batsmen I would briefly mention illustrate the emotional strain which being a batsman imposes on two opposites in character. The first, Bill Hawley (later Captain), usually withdrawn and restrained but potentially volcanic by nature, would become much less inhibited whilst 'batting'. He was conscientious and, like most batsmen, applied himself wholeheartedly to the task in hand. He took it as a personal affront if the approaching aircraft did not do precisely what he thought it should be doing in accord with his signals. The approach would commence with Bill controlled and rational, but as the aircraft came nearer an inaudible 'muttering' would be heard, with occasional expletives and, on occasions, a stream of profanity. It was not unknown for Bill to hurl his bats at the offending aircraft as it passed him. I dearly wished I could have monitored Bill's blood pressure on these occasions – I remain convinced to this day that there were instances when he was 'at risk'.

The last example is a delightful man called Algy Groombridge, a polished pilot who could make an aircraft come to life – a perfectionist. By nature he was kind, sensitive and self-effacing, and the strain of forcing himself into the dominating and demanding role of batting caused him considerable pain, which I could see was leaving a scar on his gentle personality. He had empathy with aircraft, and it offended him to see one mishandled. He would probably have made an excellent animal-trainer.

A job description for the perfect Deck Landing Control Officer might read: 'An experienced and capable pilot who knows the dangers and limitations of the aircraft he is guiding. An understanding of psychology, tolerant and able to understand the limitations of the pilots he is endeavouring to guide onto a carrier deck, especially pupils and inexperienced pilots'.

There was a large element of salesmanship required – almost a confidence trick – in that the batsman had to be able to convince the pilot that he, the batsman, was right, whether he was or not. It was not surprising that this was an area fraught with personality clashes. There was even some similarity to the doctor-patient relationship.

Whilst I was awaiting the six-week course to qualify as a

Deck Landing Control Officer, an opportunity came my way to pilot flying-boats – the Navy was still operating Sea Otters at that time, even operating them from carriers. It was a marvellous experience, providing a comfortable amalgam of seamanship and airmanship. The course was run from Lee-on-Solent and whilst waterborne we had to be aware of rules of the sea and give way to such ocean-going leviathans as the *Queen* liners, as they made their way down Southampton Water; once airborne, we had to be sort of transvestite and watch out for aircraft. One pilot with a misplaced sense of humour thought it would be interesting to display the maritime flag D on his aircraft, whilst practising taxying in the Solent. (In the International Code of Signals, D stands for 'Keep clear of me, I am manoeuvring with difficulty'.) Unfortunately when, in due course, he became airborne, he forgot to haul the flag down and returned to land at Lee. He flew past the control tower and could not understand why he was greeted at the end of the runway by two fire-engines, the station ambulance and a not-amused Commander (Air).

Soon after completing my flying-boat conversion course, my name appeared on the CW (short for 'Commission and Warrants') list appointing me to HMS *Heron*, for the Deck Landing Control Officers' course. (HMS *Heron* was a ship's name for the RN air station at Yeovilton, Somerset.) Many interesting projects were going on at Farnborough at this time, so, in order not to lose touch during the six weeks I would be away, I was able to commute daily in a spare aeroplane.

The batting course was held at Henstridge, a satellite airfield some five miles from Yeovilton. No other flying took place there, the airfield being fully committed to training already experienced pilots as deck-landing 'instructors'. For the trainee batsman to gain experience in recognizing the difference between a safe and a dangerous approach to land as would occur at sea, the rest of the pupils would fly a series of three aircraft in a low (below 300 feet) circuit, approaching the landing run in succession. Deliberate mistakes were made for the pupil batsman to recognize and give appropriate corrective signals with his bats – mistakes in height, direction and speed, even sometimes nearly stalling the aircraft. Round and round went the 'demonstrating' aircraft – they became known as 'clockwork mice'. We all took turns at mishandling the aircraft for the pupil batsman to correct. It was the only time in my Service experience when I flew without a parachute on, for if an error was made at that altitude, below 300 feet, a parachute would only have served to hinder any escape. The six-week batsman's course was completed by spending the last few days aboard the training carrier, where the procedure as practised ashore was repeated, clockwork mice and all.

I enjoyed my role as a clockwork mouse to the full, both ashore and at sea. However, the experience only served to confirm my suspicion that batsmen were, after the task of training embryo pilots to deck-land, superfluous to the act of deck landing itself. My impressions were later confirmed when I was temporarily detached from Farnborough and joined the flagship of the Home Fleet. I joined the carrier HMS *Indomitable,* wearing the flag of Admiral Sir Philip Vian, Commander in Chief Home Fleet, for the annual spring cruise to Gibraltar, where forces were joined with the Mediterranean fleet. In those days the British Joint Fleets made an impressive spectacle: four or five aircraft-carriers would be operating together, with aircraft 'cross flying' from one ship to another.

That particular spring cruise (1952) marked the end of an era. It was one of the last years when the Royal Navy could muster capital ships in strength and number almost to equal the battle fleets of the recent war. Fleets and ships were commanded by wartime national heroes: Vian (of Cossack fame – 'The Navy's here'), Mountbatten, Cunningham, Myers VC and Bennington (five times decorated commander of the submarine *Tally Ho*). To such as myself, with the sombre uniform unrelieved by the colour of war decorations, it seemed as though one was witnessing a curtain call by the Navy at the end of a splendidly performed play – in which I had played no part, so felt somewhat out of place.

I was notionally attached to 826 Squadron equipped with Fireflies but, for purposes of my researches, I also took my share of 'batting' aircraft aboard, to gain experience. This role provided me with a sentimental link with Ian Robertson, whom I had not met since he had sent me on my first solo at Gosport. In the intervening time Ian had been flying Firebrands, a particularly unwieldy aircraft due to an extremely long nose, at the front of which a large Centaurus engine all but totally obscured the pilot's view forward.

At some time Ian had attempted to land his Firebrand aboard *Indomitable* and inadvertently approached the flight deck via the batsman's platform, catching it with his hook (the batsman had vacated in terror) and turning the edge upwards in the form of a lip. Thus, whenever I was batting, especially in rough weather, I would steady myself by hooking my foot round this 'lip' so thoughtfully provided by Ian.

We also had Seafuries and Sea Hornets embarked, as well as one Sea Otter – which I was now glad that I had flown as well. Even the medical department insisted on my taking a turn of duty in the ship's sick-bay, so life was busy, and the cruise not without incident, of which two remain vividly in my mind.

The first was when I was asked to act as Carrier Air Protection (CAP) in a fleet exercise – a form of maritime 'war game'. Though I was very much an amateur when it came to hostility-style flying (shades of sheep-slaughtering on Dartmoor), I had little choice in the matter for I was an honorary member of 826 Squadron and had given an undertaking to participate to the full in all their operational exercises. I did not wish to jeopardize their tolerance, so, with Lieutenant Tony Atkins as my observer, we were catapulted one morning pre-dawn off the port catapult of the ship, in a Firefly.

We climbed up to our assigned 'station' 10,000 feet above the blue Mediterranean and some ten miles from the ship. As the sun rose in the east, the Costa del Sol was just discernible some forty miles to the north-west. Using what I thought would be an inactive piece of flying to clarify my thoughts on deck landing, I was suddenly brought back to the moment by a Seafury (an attacking aircraft) flashing by, a few feet away, followed soon after by a huge splash in the sea below and a billowing parachute above it. I heard later that two Seafuries closing upon this lone Firefly (me) sedately flying in slow circles had both pounced on me together and had collided. One crashed into the sea, the one I had seen; the pilot had baled out (without an ejection seat), and he was rescued having broken his arm; the other Seafury, being only slightly damaged, was able to make its way safely to Gibraltar. I prudently looked up the Geneva Convention relating to the role of medical officers in times of armed conflict and tactfully suggested that retaining my name on the medical register was of more importance than my competence to handle weapons of destruction. I was 'relegated' to more peaceful forms of flying for the remainder of my stay in the ship.

Even this did not remove my propensity for getting into trouble. One day in February 1952 when the ship was about 150 miles from Gibraltar I was despatched to the Rock to collect the ship's mail. Being comfortably within the aircraft's range, I took off again from Gibraltar for the return flight to the ship, without refuelling. Having found her, I saw, to my consternation, *Indomitable* becalmed and not making any visible effort to gather speed to enable me to land back aboard. I was the only aircraft airborne and, due to a misunderstanding, I had been forgotten. A signal had been received from the Admiralty ordering cessation of all exercises as a token of respect for the King, who had just died. I was brusquely told to stand off till the period of inactivity was over. By now I had not enough fuel to return to Gibraltar and was in some doubt as to whether I could remain airborne till the slumbering giant beneath me woke and gained sufficient speed to allow me to land. It seemed an eternity, but eventually I cautiously called the ship – reminding them that I had a large amount of personal mail for the ship's company. A moment's silence while I watched dejected and with increasing apprehension.

The effect was dramatic! I perceived a threshing of the sea at the carrier's stern, turning to white broken water spreading astern from the ship and, imperceptibly at first but gathering speed and turning into wind to take advantage of what little wind there was, *Indomitable* was on the move. My fuel gauges were reading near empty, and I had transferred every drop of fuel out of the wing tanks when I was flying up the starboard side of the ship at 300 feet. I looked down, saw a 'green light' indicating that I could land, and turned downwind, hook, undercarriage and flaps down, to do the tightest, quickest landing circuit of my life. It was not until after landing that I realized that, in my anxiety to get aboard before my fuel was exhausted, I had taken no notice of the batsman at all – indeed, I'm not sure that he was even there! It confirmed my suspicions that the batsman was in the nature of a 'con' trick, except for inspiring confidence during initial deck landing training.

I believe I saw confirmation of this view from another source. On an earlier occasion, when I was serving as medical officer in another carrier, HMS *Vengeance*, the commanding officer of one of the squadrons was Derek Empson (later Admiral Sir Derek Empson), arguably the most liked man in the Navy in his time. Self-effacing, a Cambridge Blue, he had previously been in charge of the

Navy Deck Landing School at Milltown in Scotland. He was thus in a position of authority to know both the value of batsman to pilots fresh to deck landing and their declining value as the experience of pilots accumulated. He also knew that batsmen were not infallible. Being a compassionate man, he had the welfare of his squadron pilots very much at heart and, when he started having trouble sleeping, I knew the growing number of lines on his face disclosed more stress than his ever-smiling face might lead one to believe.

8 *Look and Listen*

After three months in *Indomitable,* I returned to Farnborough. By this time the recognition of the importance of aviation medicine to the Fleet Air Arm was beginning to bear fruit and a third naval doctor, Surgeon Lieutenant Hugh Ford, was appointed to join us. He was rendering valuable service by helping John Rawlins to issue bone domes to all naval aircrew as quickly as possible, so I turned my attention to the conundrum of deck-landing accidents. My experience of landing on board without the assistance of a batsman when I was stranded with the ship's mail had provoked certain questions in my deliberations.

How did pilots use their eyes whilst landing aboard carriers? Jet aircraft were coming into squadron service with faster landing speeds, and there was less time to assimilate information during the final approach to the deck. I discussed it with Geoffrey Melville-Jones, still studying eye behaviour, and we continued to photograph pilots' eyes, using the camera equipment installed in the Meteor 7 – but this time photographing eyes during the final thirty seconds or so of the approach to land. The results were revealing. Sitting in the back of the Meteor, I flew with dozens of experienced pilots, completing hundreds of simulated deck landings, flying slower and nearer the aircraft's stalling speed than many of them were used to, or cared to, on the landing approach. My task sitting behind the pilot was to operate the camera and make notes on the style of approach and landing. The ensuing correlation of the approaches, frame-by-frame analysis of the pictures occupied a lot of time. Help was forthcoming in the form of two able psychologists Keith Jackson and Alan Burrows, who joined the Institute of Aviation Medicine. (Alan was provided by the Navy and eventually emigrated to California to join Al Mayo's forward-thinking team in the Human Factor Division of Douglas Aircraft, before his untimely death in the United States in the 1970s.)

A brief explanation of the physiology of vision will be helpful in understanding our results.

The complex functions of the eyes are carried out, broadly speaking, by two different types of muscles. Those enabling eye movements up, down and from side to side are, for the most part, known as voluntary muscles. They are controlled by the conscious part of the brain (with the partial exception of eye convergence – when viewing very close objects or when over-ridden by the semi-circular canals; see Chapter 5); the muscles affecting focusing and those controlling the amount of light falling on the retina by varying the size of the pupil are involuntary muscles and are controlled at a sub-conscious level of the brain, i.e. one is not aware of their functioning.

There is one important difference between the two groups of muscles – the time they take to operate. The voluntary muscles operate ten times quicker than the involuntary muscles (0.05 seconds compared with 0.5 seconds). Thus it takes considerably more time for a pilot to alter his focusing from far-off objects (the runway) to near objects (his instrument panel, air-speed instruments etc) as this is carried out by involuntary muscles. On the other hand, the change in direction of viewing (voluntary muscles) is done very much more quickly.

A second factor affecting efficient utilization of the eyes concerns how they are kept 'clean'. The eyeballs are bathed in fluid (tears) which serves to lubricate them, to facilitate smooth movement under the eyelids and also to protect them from dust particles etc. The cleansing chore is carried out by blinking, when the upper lid sweeps across the exposed part of the eyeball at an average frequency of about seventeen times per minute. To avoid interrupting the flow of visual pictures to the brain, blinking tends to take place during the moving of the eyes from looking at one object to looking at the next object to be viewed.

As our analysis of pilots' eye movements during the landing exercises proceeded, two interesting facts emerged, one expected and the other unexpected. First, as was anticipated, the only instrument referred to by the pilot during the final thirty seconds of an approach was the air-speed indicator, and even this was ignored in the final moments before touchdown. The second was that the blinking process was completely suspended during the approach and landing, but once the aircraft had touched down on the runway, this was compensated for by blinking at the rate of two or even three blinks a second, continuing for a minute or so.

We concluded that a pilot's visual pathway, his eyes, were 'saturated' during the landing phase, by a need for a constant flow of visual information relating to the aircraft's progress as it nears touchdown. Consequently other but still important data had to be neglected; thus the air-speed indicator was largely ignored as being too time-consuming to read, due, in part, to the length of time taken to refocus the eyes on the instrument. It also offered a plausible explanation why all blinking was suspended till the aircraft was safely on the ground. Two possibilities presented themselves to relieve this state of affairs: present the aircraft's speed visually as a reflection in the windscreen (head-up display), ideally projected at a distance far enough away not to require refocusing by the eyes, or use an alternative sense-receptor, the ears, which are not being fully utilized, if at all, during landing.

The RAE was already developing a 'head-up display', so we decided to explore the alternative – after all, physiologists were constantly extolling the virtues of audio-visual displays.

However, all the Lab aeroplanes were fully extended on a variety of airborne physiological experiments. The G-suit programme had been virtually completed, so the stalwart Spitfire 22 had been retired as a museum piece. The investigation as to how to combat the effects of high G had been transferred to a unique aeroplane, the Prone Meteor. This was a modified Meteor Mark 8, onto which an extended nose was built and adapted for a pilot to fly the aircraft lying on his tummy. A safety pilot sat in the normal cockpit. Only one such aircraft was built and, though not a practical proposition, it did enable the prone pilot to emerge from his high G flight comparatively fresh, compared with the safety pilot, who had to fight the effects of the G. However, this aircraft was too specialized to be of use in any other trials in the Lab. The Harvard had been replaced by a dual-controlled Balliol as the Lab's communication aircraft – with a part share in a Viking when numbers warranted. The two-seater Meteor 7 had had most of its rivets shaken out of it by the low-level pounding it had received flying over the Sahara, as had most of the pilots flying it! The Canberra was increasingly in demand for high-altitude physiology (oxygen equipment and pressure-suit development).

Thus we needed another aeroplane and, with encouragement from Pat Ruffell Smith, reasons were carefully marshalled as to why a naval aircraft was essential. We really needed a sponsor though, on the principle that a recommendation is more convincing than a request.

One morning Pat strolled into my office with an official-looking piece of paper addressed to the Admiralty. I read it with increasing astonishment and disbelief, for it began by baldly stating that the best interests of the Fleet, and furthermore of its operational efficiency, could be met only by immediately stepping up the airborne medical research effort. Whereas the results of the basic laboratory research were readily available to the Navy, the final application of such research would be useful only if tested and if results were confirmed in airborne experimentation, preferably at sea. There followed a list of various medical and physiological problems we were currently looking at, including a summary of our findings on pilots' eye movements etc, and finished with the statement: ' … that it had therefore been decided at high level that a Sea Hawk, (the latest Navy jet), should be allocated to the Institute of Aviation Medicine to relieve the pressure on the RAF aircraft already being used there'.

I asked Pat how he had persuaded high authority to plead our case so convincingly and who this authority might be. He looked at me like an old fox and said, 'You and I have just taken this decision, haven't we?' He then proceeded to remind me that, in Service memoranda, names were rarely used and that it would be unlikely that the identity of the higher authority who had made the recommendation would be questioned. Pat knew from long experience that the memorandum, if directed via the right channels, would soon turn into a bulky file with various staff observations written on it. If the initial comment does not oppose the principle, it becomes increasingly difficult for subsequent staff officers to oppose or reverse it. Thus annotations would be added to the file such as 'Good idea, but have we got a spare Sea Hawk?' or, by the less informed, 'Approve. Can the RAF doctors fly this jet?' – a poor objection. The file then becomes so voluminous that the opening phrase 'It had been decided at high level' carries the day, and it would become only a matter of time before our public relations exercise paid off and delivered a Sea Hawk into our hangar.

At that time the first naval Sea Hawk squadrons were just forming and, in due course, a signal was received that

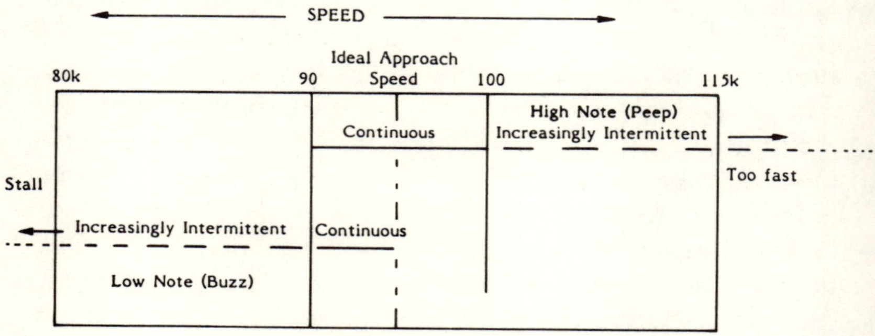

AUDIO AIR SPEED PRESENTATION

(like ordering a new car from the factory) a Mark 1 Sea Hawk, Registration No. 519, would be delivered in a few days time. The Mark 1 Sea Hawks had certain disadvantages – in particular, they did not have power-assisted flying controls, making them very heavy to handle at high speed. More significant, though, the early ones did not have pressurized cockpits – a costly omission, made without taking due consideration of the physiological requirements for operating high-performance aircraft, and a penalty I was to discover not long afterwards. (In due course our Mark 1 was replaced by an updated Mark II with power-operated controls and a pressurized cabin.)

As soon as the Sea Hawk was delivered to Farnborough, no time was lost in equipping it with the audio airspeed and various other minor experiments of a naval nature. I felt at home once more flying an aircraft in familiar naval livery with light blue under-surfaces and dark blue topside. There was one thing wrong: the arrester hook was blatantly unused – without a scratch on it, and my RAF colleagues missed no opportunity in referring to the 'land-locked' Navy. I soon found a friendly carrier working up in the Channel and paid them a visit, removing the paint from my Hawk's arrester hook in the process, rather as a bird cleans its beak on a perch. The trouble was that the land-lubber civilians who maintained the aircraft at Farnborough so efficiently took such pride in their work that they decided that the arrester hook, with broken paintwork, made the aircraft look shabby, as though it had been in an accident, and promptly repainted the hook as soon as it returned from the sea.

By this time a good deal of progress had been made towards the objective of presenting air speed in the form of coded sounds. Following a lot of research, the two psychologists had created a lab simulator, whereby subjects, mostly ETPS (Empire Test Pilots' School) pilots, responded to coded sounds representing various air speeds.

In essence the signal consisted of a two-tone buzzer. On slowing the aircraft down as it came into the landing circuit, the high-tone buzz would commence as a rapidly repeating 'peep peep', which would get slower as the speed decreased, until it became a continuous 'peeeeeeeep', signifying the speed was OK. If the speed went towards the lower end of the acceptable band (about 5 knots spread), the lower, deeper buzz would sound as a continuous note. If the speed became too slow, the buzz would become intermittent, slow at first, then with increasing urgency and volume until just before the aircraft stalled; it could be ignored only at the pilot's peril.*

* In the event, this eventually formed the basis of the stall warning device used in commercial aircraft to this day. Thus, although the audio airspeed was never fitted as standard equipment, as deck landing was becoming easier, the basic research was not altogether wasted. A similar auditory device is now fitted to the more sophisticated gliders to indicate whether the aircraft is in an up current or down current.

A prototype audio airspeed had now also been installed in our Meteor, and initial reaction from a variety of pilots was encouraging. This entailed a lot of flying to various naval stations, and we now looked forward to trying it aboard a carrier when our eagerly awaited Sea Hawk was ready.

An old friend, Nick Goodhart, later Rear-Admiral, had arrived on the scene after a prolonged stay in the USA, where he had broken three world gliding records. Nick was an engineer* and had a wide and varied experience in a great number of aircraft, including British, American and German. A deceptively genial man with an affable manner of speaking which can 'tilt' to either side of the Atlantic at will, he was responsible for developing the mirror deck-landing aid adopted widely by other navies. Nick conceived the principle whilst entertaining a girl friend to dinner, when he borrowed her lipstick and vanity mirror, using the dining table as a make-shift flight deck. His idea was to simplify deck landing to a point where landing aboard a carrier was more straightforward than landing ashore. By the pilot's keeping the reflection of a ball of light in line with two bars of light, gyrostabilized against the ship's motion, the aircraft's arrival at the correct spot on the flight deck was virtually assured. This device, together with the 'angled' flight deck, was to ensure that batting would be relegated to a place in the history books. Nick tried the audio airspeed and was encouraging.

I commenced a flying programme for the Sea Hawk equipped with the experimental audio airspeed to visit as many squadrons as possible, ashore and afloat. A wide variety of operating conditions were tried by a great number of pilots, especially at sea.

The most memorable flight I recall in the Sea Hawk was when I embarked her aboard HMS *Albion*, which was going

* His most recent achievement was to build a two-man-powered glider with a wing span greater than a Boeing 707 and was the subject of a BBC television documentary.

to the Far East, and I planned to extend the trials by using the audio air speed under varying weather conditions, including the rough Atlantic Ocean. I received approval for the Sea Hawk and myself to take passage in *Albion* as far as Gibraltar, where I would disembark and fly the aircraft home.

The outward trip was uneventful, a lot of flying carried out by different pilots, and we were pleased with the results. The carrier had 898 Squadron embarked, equipped with Sea Hawks, and the squadron commanding officer, Ian Campbell, was particularly co-operative.

I flew the aircraft ashore at the Rock and was briefed for the overland flight home. Until then the Spanish Government had refused to allow military aircraft to use their airspace but they had just relented, and my Sea Hawk was the first British jet to be given refuelling facilities at Madrid. I found the Spanish Air Traffic Control most helpful – I needed little encouragement when I was asked if I would like to make some low-level runs round the city outskirts before landing at Madrid Airport – an event for which I coaxed the maximum speed from the Nene engine. Spain was just emerging from a long period of isolation following the Civil War, so a jet aircraft was still something of a novelty. Thus my low circuit was in the nature of 'showing the flag', as I discovered many years later when I met Captain James Wood, who had been the British Naval Attaché in Madrid at that time, and it was much appreciated.

Approaching Madrid was akin to turning the clock back twenty years. Such aircraft as Junker 88s, Heinkel IIIs and similar ex-*Luftwaffe* war planes were lined up on the ground. After landing and taxying to the control tower, from habit as much as anything else I folded the wings – carrier fashion. An enthusiastic voice from the control tower gleefully announced in half Spanish, half English: 'Señor, your wings – they have collapsed.'

I was welcomed in a most friendly way and, after refuelling, I estimated that, with the help of a useful tail wind and going to maximum altitude, I could make the final leg home in one hop, as the weather over northern France was bad. I calculated that by cruising at 35,000 feet I would have sufficient reserve fuel for any diversion necessary, possibly to south-west England, which was reporting good weather. But I had not reckoned with the unpressurized cabin on the Sea Hawk.

At 30,000 feet and well above cloud I was receiving regular 'fixes' from French control zones confirming I was on track and on time. However, after being airborne for thirty-five minutes I felt the first dull ache in my right knee – akin to toothache – which got steadily worse. The aircraft cabin being unpressurized, my body was exposed to the low pressure of 35,000 feet. I was only too aware of what was happening – 'the bends', caused by nitrogen bubbles forming in the tissues due to the reduced atmospheric pressure. After a few more minutes and more 'fixes' from the French control station still confirming good progress, the pain became extreme and was spreading to other joints. I was, to all intents and purposes, a premature arthritic, a condition with which I am now all too familiar in my sixties.

I did some calculations but could not afford to descend yet to a more comfortable altitude. I felt very lonely and isolated. Mont Blanc appeared way over to starboard, poking up through an otherwise unbroken cloud cover. I supposed I could request a descent and land at one of the French military bases but was reluctant to do this on many counts – mainly for national and personal pride. I reckoned that a descent to 20,000 feet would probably keep the 'bends' within tolerable limits and was only too well aware, from working with decompression chambers, that nitrogen bubbles, if they form in the central nervous system, can simulate a stroke and even total collapse from shock. Descending to 20,000 feet would mean increased fuel consumption and would put paid to any chance of diverting from my chosen airfield, Blackbushe, near

Farnborough, where arrangements were available to clear customs etc. I therefore had to be sure that the frontal weather had cleared that area before committing myself to losing height. Whilst still trying to decide, I saw Ushant, the Channel and the last of the low clouds drifting to the east; I was clear, and called French control for a descent to 20,000 feet. I commenced going down, and by 14,000 feet the pain was beginning to ease up. As with any easing pain, the relief was most welcome. It was but a matter of minutes before I was over the English Channel, being cleared down through 10,000 feet and, soon after, touched down at Blackbushe.

Navy Flight 01 had arrived from Madrid.

9 *Welcome Aboard, Doctor*

There is a certain satisfaction about arriving aboard an aircraft carrier by air, a sense of achievement. In the early days of deck landing one was reminded of what Dr Johnson wrote about a woman preaching and a dog walking on its hind legs – that it is surprising not that it is done well but that it is done at all.

The Admiralty had been exploring the possibility of operating aircraft without undercarriages, catapulting them to get airborne and replacing the undercarriages with extra fuel to enable them to operate at greater range from base. For recovery, the concept had reached the stage where trials were taking place, using a 'rubber deck'. This consisted of a large rubber apron, approximately the size of a tennis court, stretched over rubber cylinders about three feet in diameter and filled with water. A single arrester wire was strung across one end of the deck, about three feet high. The procedure was to fly the aircraft as slowly as possible over the wire, engaging it with an arrester hook hanging from the aircraft's belly, and so be 'plucked' out of the air and bounce onto the 'bean bag'.

To be arrested from over 100 mph within the length of a cricket pitch involved a significant deceleration – of the order of 4 or 5G. Doubts were expressed as to the adequacy of the standard harness to protect the pilot from bruising, and Pat Ruffell Smith had proposed that he should participate in the trials in the light of his medical knowledge.

It was about this time that I was appointed to Farnborough, and some well-meaning person suggested that, as I had had some experience, albeit limited, of arresting procedures, I should join the trials, rather than put at risk the valuable RAF doctor. Of these political manoeuvrings I was ignorant, but presumably I was thought to be in some way expendable. So be it. I was viewed with suspicion when I arrived at the Lab. The trial proceeded with some interesting results.

It was not until some years had passed and I had been accepted at Farnborough, that I heard from Pat that, although he had flown most types of aircraft in varying roles, he had never flown aboard a ship. It was clearly expected of me to put this omission aright, and although I had no option but to accept the challenge, it was clearly a tall order.

I started my research by reading the regulations regarding deck landing, and the qualifications required for achieving this end. Admiralty Fleet Orders had clearly been drawn up by retired pilots sitting in the Admiralty, serving out their remaining days, regarding deck landing as a habit to be confined to the Navy, and outsiders to be discouraged. The impression was gained that, unless one had been recruited as a young man into the Services for the specific purpose of flying from carriers, there was little hope of achieving this end. It was conceded, though, that a limited number of civilian test pilots should be required to have such experience, and it was to this end that I directed my attention. For these pilots, required flying experience and achievements were precisely spelt out and, to my relief, no reference was made to age being a limiting factor. Scanning Pat's flying logbook revealed that he could easily meet the desired level of flying experience. Their Lordships, I recall, would be prepared to make arrangements for such pilots to undergo a course prior to being accepted for the final landing aboard ship. I hurried to find Pat, wondering if I might use my influence in the power corridors of the Admiralty to have him accepted. Pat was noncommital but when he learned the course would take six weeks, and was in the north of Scotland to boot, he blew up, saying he had not got that sort of time to spare.

Crestfallen, I returned to the Admiralty Fleet Orders (AFOs) to continue my reading as to who might or might not be permitted to take an aircraft aboard ship. The orders were quite clear. 'No one to be allowed to deck-land an aircraft unless he had completed a deck-landing course approved for the purpose, or *had already done a deck landing*.' I gazed at this latter part. It was clearly inserted originally to enable the pioneering pilots who had tried this activity before courses were in vogue to return to sea should the necessity arise.

I assessed this possibility over the next few weeks. I had been allocated the Sea Hawk at Farnborough to carry out certain experiments, but this was a single-seater, though fitted with an arrester hook. I periodically took it to a carrier, partly to remove the paint from the hook and so make it look slightly 'used'. I continued to seek a means of getting Pat to a carrier under his own control.

One beautiful summer evening I was invited to dine aboard HMS *Ark Royal*, anchored in Weymouth Bay. After dinner I was on the quarter-deck and glanced at the ship's programme for the forthcoming week, noting that she apparently had some spare time one afternoon. The captain was Denis Campbell, and at that moment he appeared on deck.

I knew Campbell, regarding him as a 'boffin' disguised as a naval officer, for he had spent many years with the Ministry of Supply. Whilst there he and Lewis Boddington had evolved the idea of the angled flight-deck for carriers, which reduced the accident rate and was adapted by the United States Navy as well as the British Navy. I knew he was amenable to outrageous suggestions, providing there was some purpose behind them, so I came to the point.

Observing that the ship was proceeding to sea in a day or so, I wondered if I might make a request, I said. He looked nonplussed, good naturedly saying that no one seemed to keep him informed. I continued. Might it be possible, by a small alteration in course, for the ship to be steaming into the prevailing wind one day later that week and, if he was agreeable, might I use his flight deck for ten minutes or so for a certain experiment? I would prefer not to go into details at this stage, I said. He looked me straight in the eye for a moment but didn't pursue the point. We both knew there was something mildly irregular afoot, but it was better not to press the issue. He agreed and moved towards his quarters, but before disappearing he turned and said, 'I suppose you want to do some "touch and go" landings – what sort of aircraft might we expect?' I explained it would be a two-seater Meteor 7 with dual controls but no arrester hook and so couldn't stop. He looked somewhat surprised but all he said was to make sure I made a signal to the ship with a copy to Admiralty – 'in case you go into the sea' – and then he was gone.

The following morning, elated, I told Pat to keep the next few days clear, as we were 'going to sea'. I explained certain matters peculiar to naval flying, including somewhat slower approaches, and we had a couple of practice trips together to accustom Pat to this unusual technique. Then the day came, and we climbed into the Meteor, me in the rear seat, with very little view ahead, and we were off, heading for the coast near Weymouth. Soon we made contact with *Ark Royal* by radio and then saw her turning into wind. As she did so, she left a beautiful white wake curling behind her as she gathered speed, informing us by radio (Pat's call sign being appropriately '99') that she was ready to receive us.

I commenced the circuit, undercarriage down, curving in to the deck, which grew rapidly larger – what I could see of it from the restricted rear seat. Over the stern, and we were down, running along the deck. Applying full power, we took off again over the bows. Once more we went in, and then I left it to Pat to try, feeling rather detached. I remember waving to the 'goofers' gazing from the bridge, and 'Flyco', and then, elated, we did three or four more landings. After we had completed our task, I made a small gesture to *Ark Royal* on a final pass, and with a 'Can't you stop? Must you go?' message from the ship, we returned to Farnborough.

When we returned to Pat's office, I noticed he was making more smoke from his pipe than usual and had clearly enjoyed himself, and we agreed that he had now 'done a deck landing'. I said we must now commence training in earnest for a sortie to sea in the Sea Hawk.

Having been fortunate enough to have qualified as a ship's batsman, I now set about training my 'pupil' for his forthcoming solo deck landing. This was done by standing at the end of the Farnborough runway making signals to Pat, flying the Sea Hawk, with my bats. 'Slower, much slower,' I kept signalling as he went round and round the circuit, practising his approaches and landings. Pat was very good, though his instinct told him that to fly so slowly was unhealthy. Nevertheless, he complied. Soon the time came when we both felt ready to go to sea.

I approached the Admiralty, explaining that it would be helpful if we might have the benefit of Wing Commander Ruffell Smith landing the Sea Hawk aboard ship 'to further his deck-landing experience'. It worked, and permission was given for certain 'trials' to take place aboard HMS *Bulwark*.

In due course Pat walked up the gangway aboard *Bulwark*, alongside at Portsmouth, and once the ship had put to sea I arrived aboard next morning with the Sea Hawk. The plan was for Pat to be catapulted off in the Sea Hawk, do a circuit, return for a normal landing and repeat this three or four times. On arrival, I observed that the fuel tanks were less than half full. (Here, a technical explanation is necessary. The Sea Hawk has two main fuel tanks, one in front and the other behind, each with a separate gauge. They empty at the same rate by way of balancing pumps, keeping the aircraft evenly trimmed.)

The moment came, after refuelling, for my 'pupil' to man his aircraft, and I accompanied him across the flight deck, feeling like a boxing coach encouraging his protégé about to go into the ring. I had a sense of foreboding. So far, we had got away with it all, but the moment had now arrived for the test. Here we were, two doctors, one elderly by most standards applicable to the situation, a beautiful day, off the south coast, aboard one of Her Majesty's aircraft-carriers, and the elderly doctor in the wrong coloured uniform for the scene.

I helped Pat into the aircraft and saw his harness adjusted, helmet on and plugged in, before taking out the safety pin from his ejection seat, and hoping I would be there to put it back again. After a few encouraging words, I patted his helmet and climbed down to the deck, which was already beginning to throb in response to the ship gathering speed as she turned, with the gentle breeze along the flight deck picking up to a gale, as if for a gathering storm. I went up on the bridge and listened to the procedure already starting for an aircraft launch. The officer of the watch was assessing the course of a super-tanker which was on the radar plot, some two miles on our port beam. The helmsman's voice acknowledged, 'Ten of port wheel on, sir.' A pause, as the great ship heeled over as the helm took effect. Then I heard 'One-eight-zero' and the whole ship started to vibrate as we gathered more speed. Meanwhile the captain was sitting relaxed on his high chair, puffing at his pipe, looking for all the world as though he was waiting for the curtain to go up at the theatre. I felt my heart miss a beat when I realized I was cast in the role of producer and this was the first night. I heard someone say, 'Hoist the aeroplane flag', and I watched the white flag with a red centre flutter up on the signal platform. Fortunately for my sense of wellbeing, I had not noticed that it had been flying at half mast till that moment. By this time Pat had started his engine, wings unfolding, flaps down, and I watched anxiously. The flight-deck officer had taken up his position just ahead and to the side of the aircraft, which was secured to the catapult, raising his green flag ready to wave him off, and leaning backwards at about thirty degrees against the wind whistling down the deck.

Suddenly a small gloved hand appeared from the aircraft's cockpit, waved momentarily and gave a thumbs down signal before withdrawing. The engine reduced from full power, and my heart sank. What could have happened? I feared the worst – had Pat uncharacteristically lost his nerve at the last moment? In the moment of anticlimax I hurried down to the flight deck and made my way to the aircraft, climbing up to see what Pat was doing. His eyes were flashing, and he pointed to the fuel gauges. I followed his finger and to my horror saw that the front gauge registered full and the rear one nearly empty! In refuelling, the flight-deck crew had put *all* the fuel into one tank. If the aircraft had taken off in that condition, Pat wouldn't have stood a chance. He would have dived straight into the sea, probably never to be recovered, and in the absence of evidence the accident would have been put down to pilot error or, worse still, inexperience. The whole story would have emerged and backlashed onto the Medical Department, and I would have been held responsible for Pat's death. Even if he survived, grave doubts would have remained.

In that single episode there was demonstrated the ability to use a sixth sense of a 'survivor'. Pat avoided any remonstration, quietly asking for the refuelling error to be rectified, and the rest of the story is without incident. He was catapulted off in due course and completed four faultless deck landings, and we returned to Farnborough.

I believe Pat Ruffell Smith was the oldest aviator, at the age of forty-four, to land an aircraft aboard a carrier for the first time.

10 *Taxi*

The 'core' of the Institute of Aviation Medicine consisted of a band of somewhat unusual medical officers, often introverts, but with two important characteristics in common – a bent for curiosity and a belief that the impossible can be made possible through determination. This combination ensured a third characteristic – eccentricity.

Most of the doctors were in the RAF, as it was administratively convenient to wear uniform, thus ensuring easy access to Service stations. It was rumoured that their wearing uniform stemmed back to the end of World War II, when a high proportion of the continent of Europe had been liberated by Allied forces. Whatever the reason, most of the doctors at the Institute wore RAF uniforms for most of the time, but their preoccupation with their research would often show up by their turning up in uniform but with coloured socks or a striped tie, habits not always immediately discerned by their equally eccentric companions.

Uniforms were the only outward sign of the Institute's being a Service establishment. There was no flag or ensign, no parade ground, no marching and little call for saluting; security, however, was of the highest order. On the rare occasions when a salute was unavoidable, the resultant sequence of events more often than not reminded me of a gynaecologist attempting to pull an open umbrella through a hawthorn hedge backwards. I felt at home.

In addition to the Service doctors there were a number of civilian doctors. One, Johnny Gabb, was with British Overseas Airways (as British Airways was then known), and his primary interest lay in survival equipment, whilst others had specialist interest in the effects of atmospheric and acceleration effects on the central nervous system. There was even a brain surgeon attached to us for a time. Supporting this team were a number of specialist civilians with expert interests in a variety of subjects from anthropology to temperature extremes.

From time to time these 'boffins' would require to make visits, often taking bulky or secret equipment, to RAF or Fleet Air Arm bases, or to consult with aircraft manufacturers. Occasionally service trials of experimental equipment were conducted overseas. Thus there was a constant call on the medical pilots, themselves usually participating in the trials, to convey these scientists together with their equipment. For these trips we would take whatever suitable aircraft was available, ranging from the two-seater Balliol up through to a de Havilland Dove to a Viking, which could take about forty people plus equipment. Though not qualified pilots, most of these Institute boffins by dint of experience became competent at handling the controls in the co-pilot's seat. This was encouraged, not only to assist the medical pilot when flying the larger aircraft but also because it gave them an insight into the problems and requirements of the operational aircrew they sought to help.

In spite of the hundreds of such ferrying flights that were made in a wide variety of aircraft, without mishap, one or two incidents cropped up worthy of recall.

One of the uniformed doctors, Peter Whittingham, specialized in aircrew and survival clothing and was anxious to conduct a trial at sea to ascertain which colour would be most conspicuous for life-rafts and life-jackets.

What was essentially a simple experiment had far-reaching effects. In the event, 'dayglow orange' was the most conspicuous colour by a very long way. The results can be seen today in a wide variety of uses where objects have to be easily seen, from life-rafts at sea to similar-coloured stripes on aircraft, and even men working on the highways, including policemen.

For the purpose of his trial Peter arranged for a number of rafts of varying colours to be tethered out at sea off the south coast. By flying on a steady course and height towards them, in varying light and sea conditions, we observed which colours could be discerned first. It was a tedious task and only fell on us as it dovetailed in with other medical work of a classified nature. We used the station communication Dove, a twin-engined aircraft designed to carry six or seven persons in comparative comfort in a cabin behind the pilot and co-pilot. It was also equipped with a chemical toilet compartment at the rear.

Peter and I had flown together a great deal and he was quite competent to handle the aircraft after take-off, though he was not a qualified pilot and had never attempted a landing. After the trials had been completed, Peter suggested he should try his hand at navigation and fly us back to Farnborough. I agreed and, to show my confidence in him, unstrapped myself and sat down in a seat in the main cabin, leaving Peter to get on with the task of flying us home, deriving considerable satisfaction from his facial expressions as he endeavoured to reconcile landmarks on the ground with the map on his knee, while I checked our progress myself.

After about half an hour it was becoming clear from Peter's increasingly agitated look that he was not so confident as to our whereabouts. We had been airborne for about two hours, so, before relieving Peter from anxiety, I stepped into the toilet compartment. I noticed a small aperture in the toilet bulkhead and peered through it, just in time to see Peter turn round to beckon me forward – only to find that, apparently, he was in sole charge of an aeroplane. The look on his face and his subsequent terror provided one of the moments that can never be erased from memory. In the event, his navigation had been faultless and all that remained for me was to take the aircraft down and land at Farnborough.

Where humans, even intelligent humans, operate levers, mistakes are bound to occur sooner or later. Either the wrong lever will be pushed or the correct one will be pushed when it should have been pulled.

On one occasion Michael Bennett, a brain surgeon attached to the Institute of Aviation Medicine for neurological research, wanted to visit a far distant aerodrome in the north as a matter of urgency to take some bulky equipment for use on an injured airman. I was asked if I could fly him there but the only aircraft available was a Viking – a medium-haul airliner in service with airlines in the early 1950s. Michael had not flown in a Viking before but agreed to act as my co-pilot, as nobody else was available. Weather reports were favourable, so we filed our flight plan, took off, climbed up through cloud and reached our cruising altitude of 8,500 feet above a layer of cloud.

Michael was keen to learn about flying in general and the operating characteristics of the Viking in particular. Having done my best to explain everything, he expressed a desire to see how well it flew with one of its two engines stopped. Happy to oblige, I explained the procedure for stopping an engine, including 'feathering' the propeller by pushing the appropriate button, which he did, and for a short distance we continued our flight with the starboard propeller motionless.

Michael understood the procedure for re-starting the engine *but* pushed the wrong feathering button, with the result that the *port* engine stopped. At the same time his anguished apology became inaudible as the generator failed to supply power to our inter-com.

I need hardly explain that my hand smacked the feathering button almost before Michael's had left it, but for a few exciting moments I was, in effect, flying a glider with the flying characteristics of a brick.

11 *The Fit and the Fit*

The justification for including this chapter on epilepsy in a book largely devoted to flying revolves around the word 'fit', which in this case has a double interpretation. The first interpretation is that one is medically fit for aircrew duties; the other in the sense of an epilectic fit, debars anyone from assuming any aircrew duties whatsoever, for epilepsy must surely rank as second only to coronary thrombosis as a cause for potential disaster in the air.

The two interpretations can, however, be neatly linked by a derivative of the word epilepsy, namely 'epileptiform' – that is, only resembling epilepsy and thus not a fit, but possibly 'fit for aircrew duties'! That is how a chapter on epilepsy came to be included in this book.

Although in the pursuit of one's medical career there are to be found many light-hearted, even hilarious, moments, epilepsy can only very rarely be regarded in this vein. Epilepsy is but one, though an important one, of a group of diseases which are far-reaching in the disproportional effect which they exert on the social, professional and working life of an otherwise usually perfectly normal, healthy person.

Reference to epilepsy can be found in the New Testament, St Luke, Chapter 9, describing an epileptic boy as being in the grip of the Devil, how he gives a sharp cry and foams at the mouth, and the practice in prehistoric times of trephining the skull to cut out the demon which had taken possession of the individual.

The more one learns about epilepsy, the more difficult it becomes to define and understand it precisely. An impression is gained that one is peering into the human equivalent of extra-terrestrial exploration and attempting to pry into the very soul of man, perhaps even linking with the largely forgotten (by humans) realm of extra-sensory perception.

Types of epilepsy range right across the neurological spectrum. There is the classic 'grand mal' epileptic fit, sometimes preceded by a warning and sometimes not, when, like a massive thunderstorm, all the available forces are unleashed in the neurological universe. Such a massive discharge of electrical energy within the brain might well be described as a 'neurological orgasm' and lasts for but a brief time, measured in seconds rather than minutes. Like a thunderstorm, it is not in itself harmful, but the results can be devastating – even, albeit rarely, fatal, as in the case of one of my patients who suffocated on his pillow during a nocturnal attack.

The massive electrical discharge in the brain during the fit puts every muscle in the body into spasm. It is this that creates the typical epileptic 'cry' which causes such distress to a witness, but none to the victim, for he is unconscious and his thought processes are in limbo. The 'cry' is caused by the respiratory muscles contracting, pulling in air through the already contracting vocal chords. Similarly the bladder may empty, with embarrassing social consequences.

Like the thunderstorm, this period quickly passes as the body's increasing need for oxygen reasserts itself. After a brief period when the arms and legs thrash purposelessly, the 'fit' passes, leaving the victim physically exhausted but peaceful, with no worse symptoms than possibly a slight headache and a desire to sleep, and no awareness of the dramatic events that have just taken place.

So much for the classic 'grand mal' attack. There are as many variants and lesser versions as there are of

A satisfactory deck landing is one from which the pilot walks away. However, this Sea Vixen hardly merited the description 'one careful driver'

HMS *Ark Royal* – an impressive vision of air power, alas no more

An unorthodox landing on HMS *Vengeance* resulting in a compression fracture of the 4th cervical vertebra and the pilot being half an inch shorter!

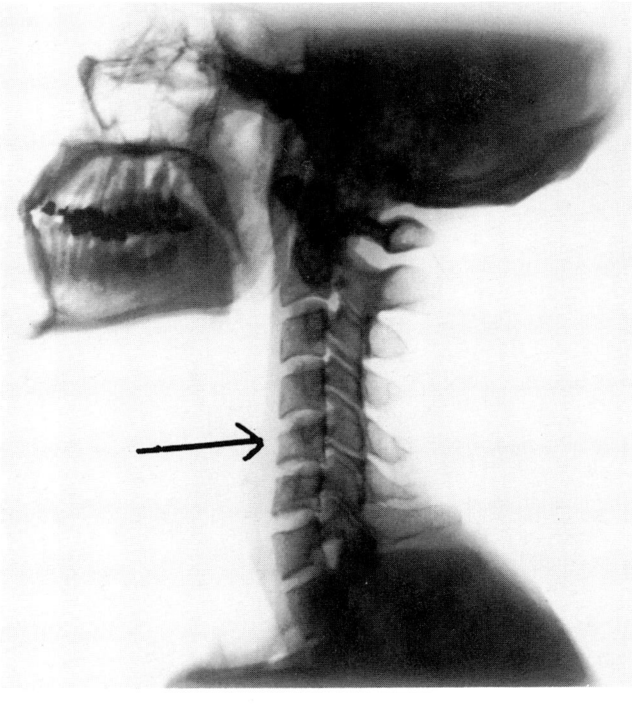

thunderstorms, right down to the cerebral equivalent of the 'northern lights', the 'petit mal' epileptic attack, lasting perhaps one or two seconds which are totally and irretrievably removed from the victim's memory. This experience can be likened to watching a movie film from which a dozen frames have been removed, leaving the viewer (or victim) to pick up the missing threads of the story as best he can. Other variants may leave conscious thought-processes uninterrupted but a limb or other part of the body may twitch or jerk, indicating localized electrical activity in part of the brain controlling that part of the body (Jacksonian epilepsy).

For all these forms of epilepsy there are, quite properly, rules and guidelines laid down, to prevent injury to the epileptic himself and to others. For example, anyone with a history of an epileptic attack cannot be issued with a driving licence unless he has been free of daytime attacks for at least two years – longer periods for 'professional' drivers and an absolute ban for certain callings (airline pilots) for anyone with a history suggestive of epilepsy. Similar restrictions prevent gainful employment in connection with moving machinery, working at heights, in dangerous positions etc. Thus a diagnosis of epilepsy should be made only after the most careful consideration, supported by exhaustive clinical investigations. The careless and misplaced application of the word 'fit' to an infant who has had a 'convulsion' whilst running a high temperature, or a bout of fainting attacks (often in themselves accompanied by 'twitching') in an adolescent, possibly under stress of examinations, should be scrupulously guarded against. Once applied, the whole course of a career can be put in jeopardy.

Lesser forms of the disease take different and often bizarre forms – for example, an attack of uncontrollable laughter. Narcolepsy takes the form of an uncontrollable desire to go to sleep. My own flying career was nearly brought to an untimely end because I would fall asleep during the ground school lectures during flying training. My medical colleague took it upon himself to diagnose me as narcoleptic, and it was only by prescribing benzedrine for myself to ensure my continued attention in class that I avoided picking up an epileptic-style tag. Notwithstanding this, I was known as 'Narco' by my fellow students, a label I was thankful to shake off after my training days.

Yet other forms of the 'neurological orgasm' stop short of a complete discharge, leaving the sufferer with some, or even complete, ability to carry out familiar tasks. He may walk or even execute complex familiar actions but be quite unaware of what he is doing or has done after he has recovered. This is known as a state of automatism and may well involve doing things which would normally be quite out of character. It is but a short step to consider whether certain cases of shoplifting by persons of hitherto unimpeachable character could be explained thus.

The only conclusion I can draw is that the study of brain function, both normal and abnormal, remains the greatest unexplored dimension in man, an area into which we have had but a glimpse.

I have selected three examples from my case notes to illustrate the diverse consequences of 'epilepsy'. There are many more similar stories which could be recounted.

'Fit to drop'

The young man who came to see me privately appeared to be a very healthy specimen physically, as I ushered him into my drawing-room, which served as a consulting-room on this occasion. He had given no indication on the telephone as to why he wished to see me but I could now see he was in a state of some anxiety.

I waved him to a chair by the fire to set him at ease and waited for him to disclose the reason for his visit. He was about twenty-one years of age, alert, with an air of enthusiasm in his eyes. He started to talk and said he had one immediate ambition – to make a parachute jump from an aeroplane – and wanted my help. I at once explained that I was in no position to grant him facilities for such a venture. He interrupted me by saying that he had access to a light aircraft from which he could make a descent but needed medical advice as to whether he should, for he had been told he might be epileptic. He had come to me as he knew I had some experience of parachuting and might understand what was involved.

I was already framing my decision, 'under no circumstances', when he continued with his story, and as we talked it was clear that, unless he had volunteered the information, I could not possibly have discovered the existence of his potential epilepsy. He had experienced what he described as a 'convulsion' when, apparently, he had lost consciousness for about five minutes. I questioned him closely. It had been a very hot day and he had not been well the previous night. He remembered feeling giddy and was sweating just before he collapsed. He had not bitten his tongue, suffered no injuries and had not voided urine. The fact that a passing first-aider mentioned the possibility of a 'convulsion' had worried him. Being a conscientious man and knowing that his driving licence required him to report any such incident to the Licensing Centre at Swansea, he did so. The official machinery had responded by suspending his licence ' … until three years had passed without a daytime attack'. (This rule has since been modified to two years.) Not being of an assertive nature and having no compelling reason to drive, he had not questioned the ruling. In any case, the three years would soon be up. I was about to suggest that he could well wait until then, when he continued.

His father, it seemed from the son's story, was of a rather dominating, though brave, disposition and had been a parachutist in World War II – he had, in fact, fought at Arnhem. He was now in the final months of his life. He was deeply attached to his son but had, perhaps tactlessly, expressed doubts about his son's courage because he had declined to dive off the high board at the school swimming baths. This incident had left a burning sense of guilt in the son, conscious of his father's heroism in the war. Now, before it was too late, he wanted to experience a parachute jump not only for its own sake but to be able to share the experience with his father.

To give me time to weigh up the implications of what I might decide, I asked him to undress and I examined him. He was in excellent health, not overweight, with good muscle tone; his eyesight and ears met all the physical standards required of an aviator or a would-be parachutist.

I made my decision. I told him there was no reason why he should not go ahead with his jump but stipulated one condition: he should jump out with a static line attached between his ripcord and the aircraft. Thus, in the most unlikely event of any mental aberration occurring in the excitement of the moment, his parachute would be opened automatically and he would complete his descent safely.

I heard later that he made his parachute jump to both his own and his father's delight and that they held a family celebration. A small decision but with important consequences. I felt a calculated minimal risk had been justified.

Topsy-Turvy Convulsion

It will be recalled that, when I first arrived at Farnborough as a surgeon lieutenant, I was relatively inexperienced as a pilot, though full of enthusiasm. The 'aged wing-commander doctor pilot', as seen through my eyes at the time, but who was of course Pat Ruffell Smith, was very clearly going to keep me in check. With hindsight he was, of course, quite right, wanting me to prove myself. Hence he arranged my indoctrination to Farnborough flying in the Spitfire as recounted earlier.

During the G-suit trials I was required to do a succession of seemingly endless tight turns, with vapour trails peeling from wing tips. That sturdy old war machine had probably spent more time flying with the accelerometer recording in excess of 4G than in normal flight. Repeated extended high G involves flying not usually experienced by pilots in routine flying. The acceleration has the effect of draining the blood from the head, causing loss of vision (blacking out) and eventual unconsciousness. The blood collects in the abdominal cavity till normal flight is resumed.

High G force has another effect: the soft tissues under the eyes, in the cheeks and under the chin are all pulled down, giving the impression of premature ageing. The RAF doctor, Johnny Howitt, from whom I took over these trials swore that his face and stomach had aged by ten years during these trials.

This phase of my early Farnborough days had two effects. Apart from gaining valuable experience, my tolerance to G was increasing and I was often asked to act as safety pilot in the back seat of the Lab two-seater Meteor aircraft whilst assessing pilots' G threshold.

Occasionally pilots were referred from Flying Training Command for G assessment. I recall one such student pilot in particular. He had a history of apparently losing consciousness due to a low G threshold.

I examined him but clinically found nothing unusual. Blood pressure, heart, lungs were all that they should be in a twenty-year-old pupil pilot. He gave a history of normal, trouble-free flying during his primary training with above-average assessments from his instructors. He continued his training in Provosts, the standard jet trainer at that time. When the time came for him to be taught aerobatics, his instructor noticed that he would 'black out' as soon as the aircraft went into a steep turn. He seemed rather nervous as he recounted the story but readily agreed to fly with me in our Meteor, which was equipped with an accelerometer for an airborne evaluation. I strapped him into the rear seat, briefing him to sit passively whilst I would fly the aircraft in carefully graduated turns, successively increasing the G and listening to his running commentary and noting how he reacted. For this purpose I usually asked my subjects to recite nursery rhymes.

We took off, climbing to 20,000 feet before putting the aircraft into a series of tight turns. I started the evaluation by pulling into increasingly sharp turns. Though my own G threshold was quite high, I realized I had met my match in this young man. He cheerfully continued through his repertoire of 'Mary had a little lamb', followed by 'Baa, baa black sheep', even to my astonishment delivering a passable singing version of 'Little Bo-peep' – admittedly a little off-key on the higher notes. Meanwhile I struggled to keep in contact with the living world by remaining silent. I tightened my stomach muscles when I found I could no longer see but could still hear this wretched recitation continuing in the back to the musical accompaniment of the two jet engines. I conceded victory to my passenger and returned to Farnborough, exhausted and nonplussed.

The problem, however, remained. Why did he 'black out' when he was flying the aircraft? I asked him to recount his early flying-training days in detail and to try to recall any untoward incidents. I was thankful for my hospital training, when the importance of careful history-taking had been stressed.

One event seemed significant. Whilst flying a Tiger Moth, a basic trainer, his personal file revealed that he had gone solo in standard time. Indeed, had already been assessed as 'Promising – takes naturally to flying.' One report, however, suggested he could be over-confident and inclined to be impatient, a common enough trait in above-average student pilots. I pressed him on this and asked whether he had attempted any 'experiments' in the air before being shown by his instructor. He admitted he had discussed the mechanics of 'looping the loop' with a fellow student and how easy it would be. He believed, then, that all one had to do was to gain sufficient airspeed, pull the stick back, close one's eyes and wait. The next time he was sent off on his own, he did just that, only to find himself 'falling out of the sky' and 'not knowing where he was for a while', reminiscent of a fledgling falling out of a nest. Birds, however, have the benefit of an hereditary flying instinct. As he told and relived this episode, I noticed that small beads of perspiration had appeared on his forehead so that it glistened. I felt we had exposed the cause of the problem and suggested we go for another flight in the Meteor. This time, however, he would fly the aircraft from the front seat and I would observe from the rear seat. I asked him to leave his microphone on so that I could monitor his reactions.

Once airborne, I handed control to my student, who climbed to a safe height. Then I asked him to do a loop. Having carried out his safety checks, he commenced a shallow dive to pick up the required speed to get us over the top, some 7 - 8,000 feet above us. It was then that an ominous sound became audible. His breathing rhythm, until then soft and regular, increased in depth and frequency. In response to his backward pressure on the control column, the nose of the aircraft started lifting up to the horizon, continuing upwards into the deep blue sky, itself darkening in hue as we rapidly climbed upwards. The accelerometer reading increased from 1G to 1½G peaking at about 2G. I was forced gently but firmly into the seat and instinctively tightened my stomach muscles to combat the G, restoring my already dimming vision to normal. I watched the back of my subject's head in front of me. He had sunk slightly deeper into his seat as the G increased. I had instructed him to commence the manoeuvre at a somewhat higher speed than would normally be required and to fly a 'wide' loop so as to allow time for observation, as I felt that this would be the moment of revelation. We were now passing through the vertical, going straight up; the airspeed was falling away, whilst the altimeter dial was racing round as we hurtled upwards.

It was, in fact, a near perfect and normal demonstration of a loop by the student, but for one thing. His breathing had by now become laboured as his lungs sucked in huge volumes of air, far in excess of what was needed or could be used by his body. Of more serious portent, however, was that all this hyperventilation was washing carbon dioxide out of his body in considerable quantities, pulling it out of the blood stream and altering the body Ph (alkalinity). The heavy panting was a manifestation of fear, originating from the almost forgotten incident in the Tiger Moth, and his subconscious mind associated this particular manoeuvre with trouble, if not danger.

Every schoolboy knows that forced heavy breathing whilst at rest causes giddiness and eventual loss of consciousness. The student pilot would soon reach this point. However, a further factor was coming into play. The G forces to which we were being subjected were also draining the blood away from the student's brain, thus depriving the brain of vital oxygen. Experiments in a decompression chamber clearly demonstrate that, when a subject breathes air at simulated altitudes in excess of about 20,000 feet, his fingers will commence uncontrollable twitching unless he breathes air enriched by extra oxygen.

As I reflected on these facts, the aircraft had reached the zenith of the loop. The altimeter was now stationary, registering 15,000 feet. The wings were level on the horizon and we were on our back. The G had eased off and the accelerometer registered half positive G. Airspeed was 100 knots. I noticed, however, that the student pilot had made no backward adjustment of the elevator trim wheel to compensate for the much reduced airspeed. Passing through the zenith of a loop is a magical moment, well known to any true aviator, when one seems momentarily to hang in space. I glanced upwards, where the patchwork quilt of the English countryside was laid out like an Oriental carpet, pattern criss-crossed by the runways of an airfield far below. White smoke was emerging from a power station like a pipe smoker lighting his own pipe.

My thoughts were rudely shattered when I realized I was lifting from my seat, whilst simultaneously the accelerometer flicked from $+\frac{1}{2}$G to -1G. The student pilot had released his grip on the control column, and the 'out of trim' aircraft hovered in the inverted position. However, my attention was directed to the front seat, where my pilot was, to all intents and purposes, in the early stages of an epileptiform-type convulsion. I could no longer hear his breathing.

It seemed reasonable not to dally too long in the rather unorthodox position in which I found my 'examination couch', as I had little inclination to set a new fashion of examining my patients upside down, besides which a patient unwittingly rendered unconscious is, I felt, entitled at least to some rudimentary first aid. I had no wish to risk a summons to attend before the General Medical Council, so I set about restoring the Meteor into a more acceptable flying configuration.

I called up Farnborough to inform them that my passenger had rather lost interest in this flight and we would be landing as quickly as possible. By the time we were on the ground, my student pilot had fully recovered and was taking a philosophical if resigned view of the earlier happenings. 'I suppose I can forget flying now?' he asked. I told him he was one of the most potentially able pilots I had flown with. I went to considerable length to explain what had happened and why. I stressed that the term 'epileptiform type' of attack was descriptive rather than diagnostic. His clearance to resume flying training would be dependent upon one further aerobatic session, which we would do on the morrow. Even if he did not feel exhausted, *I* did after the day's activities.

We talked about his hitherto unrecognized subconscious fear of aerobatics. He recounted his 'bad dreams' about 'falling off skyscrapers'. In modern jargon, we 'talked him through his problems'. I pointed out his above-average flying assessment and his high G threshold.

The next day we had an enjoyable forty-five minutes in the Meteor, he doing most of the flying, starting with a few gentle barrel rolls and working up to more complicated manoeuvres, including three perfect loops in succession, all without incident. This time, when we had finished and landed just after sunset, again I felt exhausted.

He returned to his training station, completed his course with above-average assessment and continued a very successful Service career without mishap.

A Storm is Gathering

Even before the first lightning flash on the horizon heralds the imminence of a storm, it casts its shadow across the land in a variety of ways, some clearly perceptible, others less so. A hush descends; the air becomes sultry and oppressive; animals become subdued yet restive; birds cease singing, as though unsure what to expect. A stillness descends upon the animal kingdom as though in deference to the coming fury. Other, less tangible manifestations assert themselves – humans complain of headaches. Then, with a fury unequalled by man, even in this atomic age, the gods vent their anger with an awe-inspiring display of celestial pyrotechnics, accompanied by physical unleashing of energy in the form of thunder.

So it is with the 'grand mal' of epilepsy. The victim may feel unusually well and alert when he awakens on the morning of an attack. More often, however, he will feel oppressed, ill at ease, have a headache – perhaps a feeling of numbness in a particular part of the body, providing a brief period of warning during which refuge can be sought where no harm will come when the attack breaks. On some occasions there is little or no warning of an impending attack, even to the victim. However it is not unusual for a mother, with a deep intuition for matters concerning her offspring, to 'sense' an impending attack without there being any outward visible sign to others.

So, when I was asked to see a man in his late thirties suffering from epilepsy, I paid particular attention to his story and that of his family. He had led a normal healthy life and had a good job with a happy home life, until he had had his first attack about five years previously. The attacks were infrequent, three or four a month, more of the 'petit mal' type but with a difference. He would have 'absences' when he would sit and stare vacantly, not respond to questions or spoken instructions. Occasionally he would get up and move aimlessly round the room, avoiding objects and not coming to any harm. Such a state is known as 'automatism', often following a more major attack, and the victim has no knowledge or recollection of his actions when he returns to normality. It is as though he has been hypnotized – indeed, there may well be a link between these two states.

Anti-epileptic drugs failed to control this man's attacks but they had modified the condition in rather an alarming way. He now had three or four attacks a year, instead of previously three or four a month, but now, when they came, the state of automatism might last an hour, possibly longer. More importantly, however, during an attack he would undergo a personality change and perform deeds completely alien to his character. It had been known for him to enter a shop and break glassware and china, necessitating police being called to arrest him. All this would take place without his having any recollection of his actions, after the event. Fortunately the police, on medical evidence, understood his case and tried to avoid an impasse. Of greater significance, I thought, as I sat listening to the sorry story, was the absence of discernible warning, either to himself or to his family, of an impending attack.

As we talked in the man's sitting-room in front of an open fire (a potential hazard in itself), I glanced at the large Alsatian bitch stretched out in front of the fire – in fact, right across it, effectively preventing anyone getting too close, head between her paws, as she faced her master, whom she would occasionally look at, but otherwise taking little interest in any of us.

I continued to ask about the apparent absence of warning and questioned the man as to what he first noticed as an attack developed. Without appreciating its significance, he disclosed that the first warning that anything was amiss would be when the Alsatian became restless. She would then get up and put her front paws on his shoulders, as though attempting to hold him down. In some way, long since lost to man, this animal could sense a disturbance in the form of electrical 'noise' emanating from his master's brain and which she recognized as the overture to the epileptic discharge with its accompanying danger.

12 *Go West, Young Man*

The seeds of this part of the story were sown in the first three months of 1955. For some time I had been growing aware of a certain disquiet at Farnborough. The once 'free and easy' atmosphere at the Lab was changing. The completion of the human centrifuge and the sophisticated climatic laboratory did away with much of the need to conduct so many airborne physiological experiments, perhaps the principal attraction that Farnborough held for me.

In Whitehall there was developing another phase of inter-Service rivalry – certainly so far as aviation was concerned – which made one wonder who the real 'enemy' was supposed to be! Friction flared up intermittently (and was again discernible in the 1982 Falklands incident). Perhaps understandably, it has usually been between the Navy and the Air Force and only rarely between the Navy and the Army, perhaps because historically the Navy and Army have tacitly understood that each has an equally important, traditional role to play.

It was as though the deadly and eventually harmful inter-Service rivalry that existed between the Naval Air Service and the Royal Air Force between the two Great Wars had broken out again. The reasons for the resumption of this rivalry were not far to seek. A combination of economy drives, as Britain grappled with recurring crises, and increasingly sophisticated and expensive aircraft dictated a change in emphasis in aviation medicine. Though more sophisticated, the next generation of aircraft scheduled for service in the 1970s and 1980s were not necessarily faster and higher flying, but they did call for more exacting standard of operation.

The day of the simulator was dawning, and so it was with aviation medical research. The future research requirements were not so much how to protect the aviator against greater speeds and altitudes but how to improve his performance under prevailing conditions. As simulators were created to enable pilots to complete much of their flying training without leaving the ground, so physiological experiments, hitherto carried out in the air, were increasingly conducted in the laboratory. Temperature and pressure extremes, acceleration forces (both centrifugal and linear), psychomotor tests: all could be more efficiently conducted without aircraft. More effective, yes, but inevitably less exciting.

Consequently there was proportionately less expenditure on pioneering aviation medical equipment but a refinement of already-discovered equipment. Thus the 'pioneering/experimental' field was becoming overcrowded, which tended to ferment the underlying inter-Service rivalry.

The Lab was not immune to the effect of the resulting tension, though the potentially more serious rifts were avoided by the close personal relationships which had been built up. Nevertheless there was some rivalry, which took various forms, ranging from good-natured bantering to symptoms of paranoia. A good example of the former occurred shortly after Group Captain Pat Ruffell Smith had completed his deck landings aboard HMS *Bulwark*.

During his two days at sea, Pat had noticed the traditional courtesy paid by any passing merchantmen. The ensign at the stern is dipped and held there until the senior vessel, the warship, acknowledges by momentarily doing the same, after which both vessels go about their business. Pat was a keen yachtsman and one day, sailing his yacht *Xylon* in the Solent, recognized his 'old ship', *Bulwark*, at anchor at Spithead. Mischievous as ever, he made himself 'shipshape' and prepared to sail past *Bulwark*.

Being at anchor, the officer of the watch, telescope under his arm, was pacing the quarter-deck keeping a sharp look-out for any visiting naval dignitaries. When this happened, accompanied by shouts of 'man the side', a small duty party would stub out cigarettes and emerge from cover, to give the impression to the boarding visitor that the ship's company was ever watchful and alert, before he was led below to the more welcoming glass of gin – possibly the main purpose of the visit.

Meanwhile Pat, obscured from view by the towering stern of the carrier, was approaching from the other quarter, wrestling with his red ensign, causing it to 'dip' as he passed under the stern of the warship. No response. Pat continued on his way, flag still at half-mast till he disappeared from view behind a 300,000-ton tanker.

Not one to be slighted, Pat went about and approached the carrier once more, from the opposite direction, flag still stubbornly at the 'dip' but blowing his klaxon and pointing at his own ensign. This time, success! The white ensign of the 24,000-ton ship was majestically 'dipped' in acknowledgement to Pat's salute.

As a bonus *Bulwark* gave two blasts on her siren, a personal acknowledgement of Pat's presence.

The more extreme form of rivalry could be damaging, disclosing an insecurity in those involved. I was saddened and mystified when, one day shortly after the V-bombers had come into service and were Britain's then officially designated nuclear deterrent force (before the Polaris submarines), Peter Whittingham was at pains to point out that *now* the RAF was the senior Service. As if it mattered in the final analysis!

In general terms, the combined forces of the American

aircraft industry, backed by unmatchable US Government resources, were outpacing the British in the design and development of airframes, though the British were holding their own in engine design, which included the vertical take-off field. For a time, the ill-fated Comet Mark I looked as though it might mount a challenge in the commercial jet class, about to open up mass passenger travel, but for a new threat – metal fatigue. I mention this because of a little-known piece of physiological evidence which helped to solve the mystery of the first Comet crash. A brief reminder of what happened could be relevant, as physiology had a part to play. The full facts have been well documented elsewhere.

On two separate occasions a Mark I Comet bound for London from Rome was lost in mysterious, but similar, circumstances. Each aircraft fell into the sea about half an hour after taking off from Rome, all on board perishing. The salvaging of the wreckage is a story in itself, but salvaged it was, and brought back to Farnborough piece by piece, identified and re-assembled in the appropriate position on a wooden mock-up of a Comet I.

Apart from the structural recovery of the wreckage, a number of bodies had been recovered from the sea – in varying degrees of nakedness, the clothes having been torn off by sheer force. It was noticed that the exposed parts of these bodies were 'sunburnt'. The first conclusion was that, in some way, the aircraft had made a controlled 'ditching' and some of the passengers had escaped, still living, only to perish later – perhaps from sun stroke.

This hypothesis was difficult to reconcile with another known fact – namely that there was evidence of a fire somewhere in the aircraft, as a portion of one wing was blackened and, because of the pattern of the scorching, that this had taken place before the aircraft came down in the sea. However, when the broken portions of the wing were brought back to Farnborough and re-assembled in the appropriate place on the wooden mock-up, it was

The author finds an old friend at RAF Museum Cosford. An experimental Avro 707 built to evaluate characteristics of the later Vulcan bomber. (Note the prone Meteor in the background)

Cody's Tree at Farnborough to which that early aviator is supposed to have tethered his aeroplane

The last launch (followed from the steam catapult by the wardroom piano) . . .

. . . and HMS *Eagle* goes to the breaker's yard (1974)

found that the outboard portion of one wing was uncharred, with a clean cut-off point separating it from the charred portion next to the aircraft fuselage. This indicated that the aircraft had broken up in the air and that the fire had scorched the remaining part of the wing after the break-up. The 'ditching' had been violent, with no possibility of survivors. Given this sequence of events, the occupants must have perished either before or immediately on impact with the sea. How could this be reconciled with the finding of 'sunburn' on the bodies, hitherto thought to be an ante-mortem chemical change in the skin? Research revealed that, just as certain metabolic activities such as the growth of hair and nails continue for a time after clinical death, so some chemical processes continue – including 'sunburn' if the body is exposed to the sun's rays.

One piece of evidence, in particular, indicated that the aircraft cabin had exploded at altitude, ejecting the passengers through a hole in the fuselage. The imprint of an Indian coin was found on the leading edge of the fin and rudder, where it had been struck by the ejected contents of a passenger's pockets – the aircraft had originated its flight in India, stopping at Rome for refuelling.

The cause of the explosion was traced to a hair-line metal crack in the corner of one of the passenger windows.

These two tragic incidents set Britain back in the race for ascendancy in the commercial jet age and opened the way for the big American jets to attain what turned out to be an unassailable position, in spite of brave attempts to regain the lead with the VC 10 and that technically magnificent, if commercially controversial, aircraft, Concorde. Apart from these two notable exceptions and, lately, certain military aircraft developed jointly with her Common Market partners, Britain has tended to excel in aircraft engines rather than airframe design.

These and other trends were influencing my thoughts in my later years at Farnborough when a happy stroke of luck came my way which was to mould the pattern of the next few years in my Service life. I felt that I had given as much as I was able during my stay at Farnborough. I was getting stale, outgrowing my ability to keep up to an acceptable standard, for me, for matching the increasing performance of the next generation of aircraft. I was by now in my mid-thirties, and it was time to move on. But where to? The Naval Medical Department was getting restless and making noises about getting me back to sea in the sick-bay of a carrier, where I knew I would do little but dispense pink pills to pale people and too much pink gin to myself.

The stroke of luck came in political form. At that time, 1955, the West had not 'officially' recognized the source of the real threat, though it was obvious for all to see – Russia. It was decided to mount a small team (dubbed the High Performance Research Team) to visit the United States, to find out American thinking on the threat and how, and with what, the Americans would meet it. Being essentially orientated towards aviation, the team consisted of an RAF engineer test pilot, a New Zealand Air Force officer with special knowledge of equipment and, in recognition of the vital role the human pilot would play, an RAF medical pilot, Alan Crawford. When the Admiralty got wind of this, representations were made for the Navy to be represented, and I was nominated to join the HPRT. Because of the scope of the exercise, we were given very positive security vetting – a new experience, and off we went to America for six weeks, on what turned out to be a most revealing trip. The Americans were quite superb and within the permit of our high security clearance, withheld nothing. We first visited their Intelligence centre, the Pentagon, where the anticipated scenario for the ensuing decade was unfolded. Though it is public knowledge now, it was frightening in the extreme at the time to us in our privileged position.

We visited the various command headquarters, Strategic

Air Command, to see how the generals would cope with crises should they arise, and aircraft manufacturers, to hear what designers might be able to create in terms of aircraft and what hostile environments this might entail for aircrew. Included in the itinerary were visits to equipment designers and a preview of an early concept of space garments. Training procedures were included, and possible ways to experience zero gravity. It was infectious to perceive the professionalism with which the Americans approached any project, of whatever size.

We travelled the length and breadth of the United States from Washington DC, where we mingled in the diplomatic set, with naval and air attachés, to California, where the advanced thinking took one's breath away. It was there that I visited the Ryan Corporation at San Diego, whose founder built the *Spirit of St Louis* in which Colonel Lindbergh flew the Atlantic.

Another display impressed me at Patuxent River, in Maryland, when I was shown a blind landing system and, sitting alongside the pilot, saw a demonstration landing carried out without touching the controls. This was in March 1955.

These two events served to destroy the myth that the British conceive ideas which are then developed by the Americans. The Ryan vertical take-off aircraft never came to anything, but its equivalent, 'the Flying Bedstead', first flown by Ken Hough at Farnborough, was developed by Hawker Siddeley and turned eventually into the Harrier in the hands of that perfectionist pilot Bill Bedford. The second prototype was developed into an automatic landing system and used in a commercial aircraft, the Trident, by the British many years after the Americans had pioneered the principle.

The brief tour also included Pensacola in Florida, the Naval Training Centre, and Dayton, Ohio, where Colonel John Paul Stapp was still collecting data from his record-breaking (600 mph) rocket sledge runs, and then directing the United States Air Force Medical Center. When the time came to return home, I knew I wanted nothing else but to move to America and rekindle the enthusiasm and excitement which somehow seemed to have been replaced at Farnborough by inter-Service bickering and by threatened Defence cuts by HM Government.

In addition there were rumblings born of the coming 'technological revolution', with officials in 'high places' darkly hinting that pilots would be replaced by black boxes. It was this line of thinking that made Pat Ruffell Smith announce his view to the contrary in a forthright lecture. He asked how such an efficient adaptable computer (the pilot) could be produced weighing about 180 pounds and turned out in such numbers for so little cost by unskilled labour – and, as a bonus, be such fun to make!

Before leaving Washington I had received an unofficial invitation to spend two years on loan to the US Navy. It came at the right moment. I had had a good innings at Farnborough, but the excitement was lessening. I was aware, none the less, that I had been both fortunate and privileged to have been there during the 1950s, a vintage decade for British aviation, when Farnborough had been the focal point for the testing of a new generation of aircraft. Pilots from the Royal Navy and Royal Air Force, with their civilian counterparts, had accepted the challenge to evaluate the many prototypes to their design limits, and sometimes beyond, together with attempts to divine the parameters of human tolerance to fly them. The team at Farnborough was closely knit, and this, together with the civilian ground crew and the Air Traffic Controllers' empathy for each pilot's capability, made for a high degree of flying efficiency not seen since Battle of Britain days, and which would be hard to match today.

Now my heart and interest were already turning to the West, and I was impatient to receive my anticipated appointment to serve with the United States Navy. However, as with all official projects, it took some time to obtain official sanction for my transfer. Also in the inevitable file which developed on my appointment, my name probably got confused with that of Surgeon Captain Frank Ellis, a British naval doctor who had made a considerable reputation for himself as an expert on ships' environments and on the effects of working in high temperatures and high humidity conditions. (He was a prolific writer on his subject, and rumour had it that such was the length of his thesis for his Membership of the Royal College of Physicians that the examiner weighed it rather than read it.)

I had hoped to be attached to the US Navy School of Aviation Medicine at Pensacola in Florida, where there was work being carried out not dissimilar to that I had been doing at Farnborough. In addition, Pensacola was the centre for naval flying training, and I had little doubt that much flying would have been available. In the event, however, when my appointment had been mulled over between the Admiralty and the Pentagon, I was ordered to report to the US Naval Air Defence Center at Johnsville, near Philadelphia, 'for duties at the centrifuge'. My heart sank! This particular centrifuge was, naturally, being American, the largest in the world. It had a single gondola suspended at the end of the counter-balanced arm of fifty-foot radius and was capable of exposing human subjects to a sustained acceleration of 30G.

I awaited my passage with foreboding. My despondency was not dispelled by the sight of a vast armada of ships assembling in the Solent – clearly visible on my flights from Farnborough when we were doing trials involving flying over the sea. It was 1956, and forces were being assembled for Suez.

By the time I sailed from Southampton in RMS *Queen Mary*, the armada had dispersed but the Suez conflict had begun, with attendant strain on Anglo-American relations.

During the six-day crossing, while I had only the ship's newspaper from which to glean information, trans-Atlantic relations reached a low point unequalled for many a decade. When I arrived at Johnsville (about which I was still despondent), I found I was professionally unacceptable and socially undesirable in American circles, which made me very sad, as I was, and still am, a great enthusiast for the American way of life.

Meanwhile I took stock of my position. The big human centrifuge was housed in a sombre, round building made of reinforced concrete, the main part of which contained offices (in one of which I was given a desk), for the most part bereft of windows, with forced air conditioning. The reason for the absence of windows became clear when the giant centrifuge ram was engaged and the whole building rocked and shook like a ship in a force 11 storm. That was the impression I had, sitting in my office, with steel furniture, which did little to lighten my gloom.

The research director of the centrifuge was Dr James Hardy, a civilian physiologist and a captain in the US Navy Reserve. There was also a regular US navy doctor, Captain Herbert Shepler, in charge of military experiments.

Though my new colleagues were the model of courtesy and personally friendly, it was abundantly clear that my presence was an embarrassment on a base where much of the work was of a classified nature, during a period of diplomatic coolness emanating from Washington over the Suez affair. My own position was not helped by the British Joint Services Mission in Washington making it abundantly clear that I was on my own and had to make the best of it, being wholly under the direction of the United States Navy.

I reflected that I had often thought that the best time to approach traffic lights is when they are at stop – the position can only improve. This was certainly the position which greeted my arrival at Johnsville.

The centrifuge was situated at the Naval Air Development Center, which was host to a number of research laboratories. There was a small airfield which provided limited flying facilities, largely of a communications nature, but also there were one or two naval combat aircraft. At that time one of the largest computers (code-name 'Typhoon') was available for aviation research. The computer laboratory was directed by Commander Fink Fischer, an eccentric engineer who had been passed over for promotion, was still actively flying and didn't give a damn for authority. If he took to a person, that person was a friend for life. Fortunately he took to me (and he is still liable to turn up unexpectedly at my home, arriving in his own aircraft, though he is now approaching his seventieth birthday). He was to be my saviour.

Meantime there was nothing to do – or, to be precise, nothing I was allowed to do. I shared an office with a non-medical physiologist, Lieutenant-Commander Frank Burgess, who became a close friend but who was embarrassed by the political impasse. Our friendship tended to flourish out of business hours, fuelled by vast quantities of duty-free liquor to which I had access from Washington. This did more towards strengthening Anglo-American relations than anything else to which I had access!

For many weeks there was little I could do but read *The Times* in my vibrating office. I was able to enhance my growing reputation as a Britisher with a dry sense of humour by giving selected readings from the Personal Column of *The Times*. The Americans could not believe that we conducted our affairs in such a manner. Frank would periodically appear, clad in experimental flying-clothing, with a built-in anti-G suit, trailing electrical wires, and the whole building would periodically shake as the centrifuge would thunder round – it was like being at the epicentre of an earthquake.

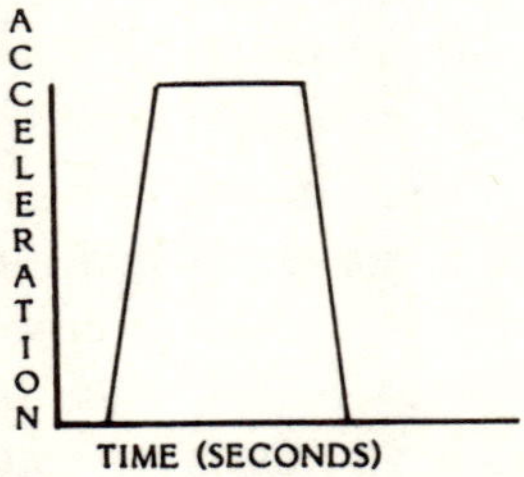

1. ENGINEERS' OPTIMUM ACCELERATION PATTERN, NOT ACCEPTABLE TO THE HUMAN FRAME

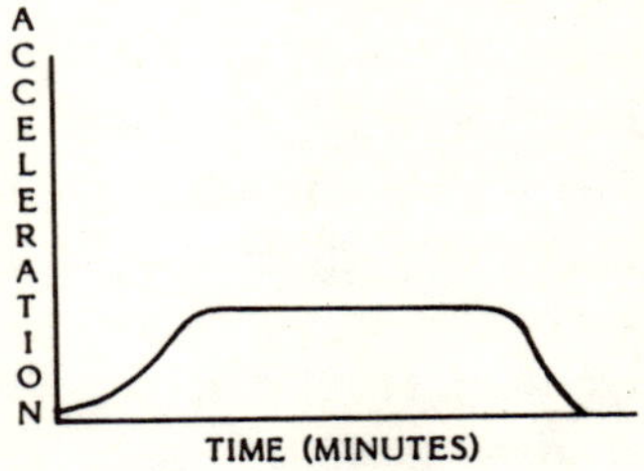

2. PHYSIOLOGICALLY ACCEPTABLE PATTERN

After a few weeks spent in inactivity, I started to explore. It was generally known that the Americans were particularly interested in two fields of space exploration at that time. Both were widely reported in the press, and only the details were restricted, though released subsequently.

One of the experiments was designed to define the upper limits of acceleration sustainable by man on an extended basis, over half a minute. The practical application of this was how to determine what acceptable combination of extended high levels of G would enable man to achieve 'escape' velocity and so get into space and orbit the Earth. The rocket engineers would have found it convenient to apply an 'explosive' force for a brief time.

The other experiment was the forthcoming flight of the X-15 aircraft. This was designed to break out of the conventional manned aircraft flight envelope which was generally restricted to some 75-80,000 feet in height and about Mach 2 in speed.

It was largely resulting from these two experiments that accelerations built into the Apollo programme were approved, and it might be said that the Space Shuttle is also a descendant of the X-15 project.

To determine the absolute tolerance of living creatures

to accelerations, it was inevitable that some animal experiments were performed, and for this purpose a small number of chimpanzees were kept in large, airy cages in the animal section behind the centrifuge. To pass the time I would visit the chimps, feeding them with occasional titbits, and we became, in a sort of fellow-suffering way, 'attached'. I observed that they were astute enough to notice that, when one of their number was taken away to the centrifuge, he or she did not return. They developed an antipathy towards one keeper which was quite extraordinary to perceive. They would gather together in a group in a corner, chattering, and one day I was astonished to see one of them, upon this particular keeper's arrival inside the cage, crouch down, defaecate into its hand and suddenly throw the dung straight at the keeper's head. This incident was repeated on other occasions until, eventually, the keeper caught the dung in his hand and threw it back at the chimp, with rather better aim. The chimp never did it again.

As the experiments of high G continued, I realized that the number of chimps was steadily declining and would soon run out. I knew from Captain Hardy's muttering that he had overspent his budget for the year, so I seized my opportunity. Why not, I said to him, now that sufficient data had been collected, start to replace the chimpanzee experiments with humans? Unknown to me, a civilian physiologist attached to the lab, Flannagan Gray, had already drawn up a human experiment. My proposal appealed to Captain Hardy, and my name was added to the list of human subjects to be used on the centrifuge trials. Thus I always felt I was allowed to stand in for the last of the chimps.

Frank Fischer was also beginning to take pity on my position and went to considerable trouble to get me cleared for flying US Navy aircraft. In typical American fashion, once the difficulties of Suez evaporated I was encouraged to fly whatever aircraft might be available.

One could not but be impressed with the high degree of professionalism with which the US naval pilots set about their flying, with thorough checks on ability at every stage.

I was particularly impressed by the approach of the naval authorities towards flying. They seemed positively to encourage flying on any occasion, even for leave purposes, presumably on the principle that an aircraft in the air was encouraging aviation 'thinking' much more than one in the hangar.

To this end the base regulations permitted a Service-qualified aviator to take a communications aircraft, if available, to any base in the USA within a thousand-mile radius of Johnsville. This gave great scope not only to broaden one's knowledge of America but also to gain experience in flying the American airway network. I made many of these flights with Fink Fischer, whose standard of airmanship was equivalent to that of a commercial pilot, so that, if weather conditions were adequate for the airlines to fly, he would be filing his own flight plan.

Fink and I flew many thousands of miles together all over the States, usually at night (Fink's choice, as he said he got confused by seeing the ground terrain!) and in a variety of climatic conditions. The most hazardous trip was when we flew in a twin-engined Beechcraft aircraft to a Strategic Air Command base in Maine and took the opportunity of collecting some live lobsters, which were placed in the otherwise empty passenger cabin. We made the return trip to Johnsville by night (by this time I was never without a torch whenever I left home) and ran into some rather turbulent weather for a short time. After emerging from cloud into clear weather, with a beautiful full moon straight ahead, I became aware of an unusual 'clicking' sound in addition to the regular engine noise. I looked at Fink alongside me. He was as usual engrossed in his voluminous air navigational direction books. He was partially deaf and had not heard anything unusual. I searched around. The engine instruments did not indicate anything untoward.

Meanwhile I fancied I noticed that the clicking had intensified and seemed nearer to hand. Something made me glance over my shoulder, and I can still feel the cold shiver that ran down my back. There in the cabin behind us, eerily discernible by the shafts of moonlight shining through the cabin window, were the lobsters, their black shells shining, claws agape (they had not been tied), wandering all over the cabin floor. They must have escaped from the cardboard boxes in which they had been placed for the journey. Fortunately they were prevented from making their way onto the flight deck by a twelve-inch 'sill' separating us from the passenger compartment.

We continued our flight gingerly, taking good care not to execute any unusual manoeuvres and with extra caution on landing. The aircraft was subjected to a particularly thorough post-flight inspection.

13 *'Give It a Whirl, Herb'*

Thanks largely to Fink Fischer's efforts in getting me cleared to fly American Navy aircraft, the post-Suez estrangement was soon forgotten, though a considerable amount of time had been wasted and nearly half my two-year appointment was to pass before I was to participate in any useful research.

The number of available chimpanzees continued to diminish but Flannagan Gray was nearly ready to carry out some preliminary runs on the centrifuge. Flannagan was of Irish descent and had little or no regard for his own safety. He was dedicated to experimentation in the field of acceleration to the point of eccentricity, and for some years his name was in the *Guinness Book of Records* for his having been exposed to the highest G force for the longest time – during the acceleration experiments conducted on the Johnsville centrifuge.

Flannagan's primary objective in his experiments was to be achieved in fundamental basic research, to ascertain what level of sustained G a body could withstand in an unprotected state. From 'unprotected' experiments, it was known that the body, immersed in water, could withstand very high G forces without loss of consciousness. It was also known from centrifuging goldfish in water that, though they could survive G forces measured in hundreds rather than tens, their balancing organs were destroyed and they were unable to swim the right way up. Autopsies on some of the chimpanzees which had been 'spun' (anaesthetised) up to 30G unprotected by water showed evidence of internal haemorrhages and critical damage to certain vital organs.

Armed with this knowledge, we started a series of runs on ourselves. The 'gondola' at the end of the centrifuge arm looked something like a bathysphere. It was attached to the arm by means of gimbals, to enable the acceleration to be directed to the body on a constant plane – rather like an amusement-ground roundabout. It had no windows, so all the interior of the gondola, and any instrumentation required for the experiment, was brightly lit. The 'subject' was strapped into a pilot's seat as in an aircraft. Two-way voice communication was maintained with the centrifuge control room throughout. The subject had the ultimate control over the centrifuge operation through a 'dead man's handle' principle in the form of a switch – if he failed to keep it depressed, it would break the main circuit and the centrifuge arm would be brought to a halt. The only concession Flannagan would allow as protection was an inflatable anti-G suit which served to defer the onset of blacking out or even unconsciousness as the higher G forces built up.

There were still a few experimental runs using chimpanzees, but at comparatively low G levels, to measure heart-rate changes for different postures, and I swear the chimps welcomed human participation in their experiments. On the other hand, they were not always continent, and I can still recall the smell inside the gondola following a chimp on a run. I dare say the chimps were not completely happy at following a human in the gondola either.

Scientific details of the Johnsville centrifuge experiments have been fully documented in scientific journals in a style to which I do not aspire. I can only record my own impressions.

A run on the centrifuge is a unique experience. After

strapping in has been completed and after one has donned special undergarments, dozens of wires are attached to one's body to record respiration rate, heart beats, blood pressure and, in some experiments, eye movements, as well as an electro-encephalograph. Next one puts on an anti-G suit, flying-helmet and flying-suit, before being led to the metal gondola to be plugged in.

When the heavy metal entrance door clanged shut, I felt very isolated. First there was silence, except for the low hum of the air supply, then the reassuring voice in the head-set of the centrifuge controller, as he checked all the systems, much as a pre-flight check before take-off might be done, including – I was glad to note – the satisfactory operation of the 'dead man's switch' giving me ultimate control over my own destiny.

Then, checks completed, came a voice in my ears, loud and encouraging: 'OK to go? Right, give it a whirl, Herb', followed by a smooth start not unlike a tube train pulling out of a station – with one important difference. At the moment when the train might have entered the tunnel at the end of the platform, the gondola tipped, on its gimbals, onto its side to keep the G force in a constant plane relative to the body. As the giant arm of the centrifuge moved, one's whole body was forced into the seat, and the accelerometer needle moved steadily round the dial as the gondola thundered round and round and round. A sudden punch in the abdomen, and one's legs were gripped as though by a python, confirming that the G valve had been activated, pushing compressed air into the anit-G suit bladders protecting one's stomach and legs. The effect was similar to a supercharger tripping in to assist a flagging engine, in that the heart, already failing under the strain, was given back-up assistance to push the blood round the brain just in time to restore failing vision and ebbing consciousness.

At 6G the gondola steadied for some fifteen seconds before slowing down, the pressure relaxed, followed by a slight clunk as the gimbals gently restored the gondola to an upright position and the arm slowed to a halt at the loading platform. I felt hot and sweaty under the powerful arc lights until the metal door was opened and I was released.

That was my initial introduction to a trial run to accelerations induced in a controlled laboratory situation. I recalled the early days of the airborne experiments in the veteran Spitfire at Farnborough. We had come a long way, though the somewhat smaller human centrifuge at Farnborough had not then been brought into service.

Soon after that, Flannagan's experiments got under way in earnest, involving up to two or three runs per subject per day. Each run, including preparation would take about an hour, and the actual run with G being applied would last from half a minute (for the higher forces) to five minutes at lower levels. The latter were quite tolerable, as has been shown in the subsequent experience of humans in space. The shorter-duration, higher-G runs soon showed up the limitations of the human body: inability to stand upright without support after completion of the run, resembling a drunken man. By the time 12 and 14G were reached, there was evidence of small haemorrhaging – especially in the eyes. As the runs continued, the giddiness would last longer, and some permanent disturbance to the body's balancing mechanism manifested itself. Even today I always leave a nightlight on, to avoid toppling should I have to leave my bed during the night (increasingly frequently!). Whenever I see a goldfish, I feel a bond between us and peer at it to make sure it is swimming the right way up. In recent years my impromptu staggering has attracted the attention of over-zealous policemen on more than one occasion.

The second major series of experiments in which I was allowed to participate were much less in the nature of brute force and, to me, more interesting as they consisted of simulating certain aspects of the flight configuration of

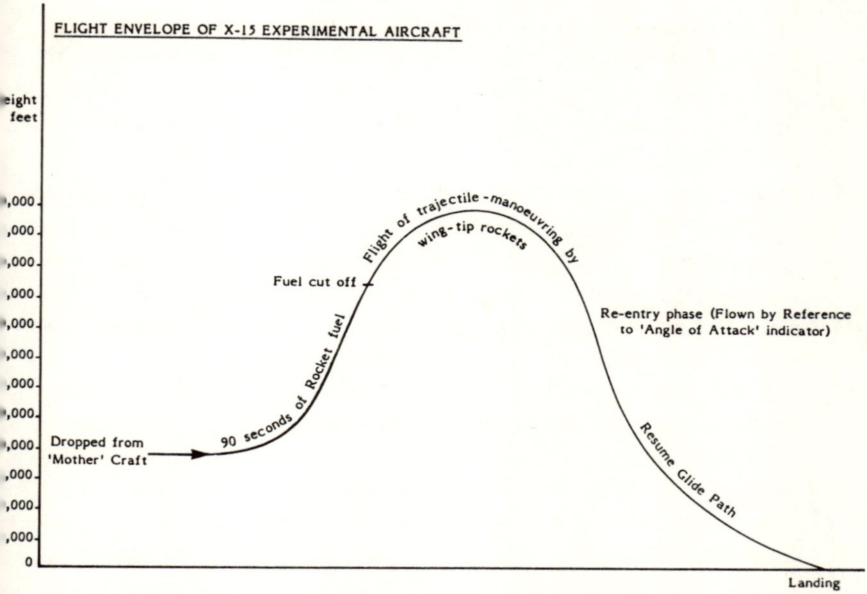

the X-15, the latest in the X series of experimental aircraft designed for supersonic flight.

Unlike earlier aircraft in the series, the X-15 was rocket-propelled, and it had sufficient fuel to drive its rocket motor for only about ninety seconds. To launch it, the aircraft was slung beneath the wing of a 'mother' aircraft, which would take off with the pilot already in the X-15. On attaining the required altitude, the X-15 pilot would ignite his rocket motor and detach from the mother aircraft to commence his independent flight. This could take one of two forms, either accelerating to a supersonic speed more or less in level flight or pulling up in a steep climb rather in the manner of a porpoise leaping out of the sea, into the upper reaches of the Earth's atmosphere, too thin to support conventional flight. It was this second flight pattern which was to be simulated at Johnsville. After either of the two flight patterns the X-15 would glide back to land on the desert landing-strip where the flight had begun.

The purpose of simulating the 'porpoise leap' version of the flight in the centrifuge was to reproduce the acceleration forces likely to be met during the 're-entry' part of the 'Flight' into the Earth's atmospheric envelope. A mock-up of the X-15 cockpit was installed in the centrifuge gondola with a full instrument panel and controls. By means of a link-up with a computer, the centrifuge would react by exerting the appropriate G forces in response to the pilot's controls, adjusted for the altitude and flight configuration. At the same time the instruments in the simulated cockpit would give the appropriate readings. Thus a standard X-15 simulated flight would run in the following way.

One of the four 'pilots', including two of the X-15 test pilots, 'Chuck' Yaeger and 'Scotty' Crossfield, would be strapped into the gondola wearing appropriate flying-gear, including an anti-G suit. At the commencement of the flight (detaching from the mother aircraft) the centrifuge would remain still but the pilot's instruments in the gondola would respond by showing a change to a nose-down attitude of the aircraft, and a simultaneous loss in altitude.

As the pilot ignited his rocket motors to commence his ninety-second powered flight, the gondola would tip on its gimbals as the centrifuge arm rotated, at first slowly, then increasing in speed, and so exerting more G on the pilot as he pulled up into a near-vertical climb. As the 'altitude' of the simulated flight increased, the computer made the pilot's controls increasingly sluggish and unresponsive to the rarified air. After ninety seconds, when the rocket motor stopped, the centrifuge arm would stop rotating (the aircraft in reality being in a zero G – weightless – condition, not possible to reproduce on the centrifuge), but the instrumentation would continue to show a continuing climb towards the peak of about 120,000 feet. During this stage of the 'flight' the conventional controls had no effect, and the 'pilot' had to keep the aircraft in the required configuration by 'bleeping' small rockets and so applying corrective forces in the rolling, pitching and yawing planes, with constant reference to his instruments, the whole being accurately portrayed on the gondola's instrument panels.

After rolling over the top of the trajectorial flight path, the pilot had to ensure that he 're-entered' the dense atmosphere at the correct angle – too steep, and the aircraft would go into an uncontrollable dive at too high a speed, from which recovery would be impossible; too shallow an angle, and the aircraft would 'skip' along the Earth's atmosphere – in the manner of a flat stone skipping across the surface of a pond. Finally the angle of 'attack' or incidence, at which the stubby wings would 'bite' the denser atmosphere, had to be correct, to avoid a stall, and for this an angle-of-attack instrument and an accelerometer were the key instruments. These had to be placed near the centre of the pilot's visual field to avoid his losing sight of them during any 'greying out' under G loadings during the re-entry phase. (Under G loadings, the peripheral fields of vision are lost before the central part.)

It was during this re-entry phase that the centrifuge came into its own. Movement of the controls by the pilot were deceptively unresponsive at the peak altitude but, as the altimeter unwound – increasingly rapidly – so the centrifuge came to life, applying sometimes vicious forces to the pilot's body as he moved his controls. If, as frequently happened in the earlier runs, the pilot caused a pre-determined G limit to be exceeded, a safety circuit would be activated and the 'flight' would be terminated by the gondola's being brought to a juddering halt signifying a crash. To emphasize to the pilot the seriousness of his actions, the gondola would, as often as not, finish in a position whereby he was left hanging upside down in his harness till rescued.

This series of experiments lasted several months and

took up much of my detachment period at Johnsville. I was impressed with the determination and thoroughness displayed by American researchers, backed up by resources of a magnitude unlikely ever to be available in Britain. In spite of the often brash image portrayed by America, one could not fail to admire the quiet, unassuming way in which ground and airborne experimentations – often of a dangerous or potentially harmful nature – were tackled.

The Americans as well as the British were interested in the tactical advantages of low flying and had heard of our experiences at Farnborough with the buffeting sustained by the Lab Meteor (see Chapter 4). It was natural that the US Naval Acceleration Laboratory should be asked to look into this problem, and I was drawn into the discussions and quizzed on how the wing rivets had 'popped' from the Meteor, giving it a battle-scarred appearance.

The American approach to investigating the problem was much more fundamental than the British, and approval was sought to simulate, in a controlled laboratory situation, the oscillations likely to be encountered during low-flying runs. It was proposed that this should be done by building a platform capable of being shaken vertically up and down through heights varying between a few millimetres (for high frequencies) and a metre, and so reproduce a wide range of 'shaking'. A pilot's seat was bolted to the platform, and 'volunteers' were strapped onto the seat like hunks of meat straight from the abattoir.

I knew enough to realize that various parts of the body and specific organs within the body respond if they are exposed to their natural resonating frequency and can suffer damage if exposed to that frequency for too long, very much as a glass will shatter if 'sung at' by a powerful opera singer. Similarly, it is a long-practised military precaution to order columns of marching soldiers to 'break step' on crossing a bridge as the combined weight and simultaneous 'stepping' of such a body of men can set the bridge shaking rhythmically and eventually make it collapse. Similar results can be obtained in various parts of the body. Indeed, the microwave oven is an extension of the same principle. I hasten to add that no plans were laid to expose our subject to *those* frequencies.

One can demonstrate the same 'vibration principle' by taking a half-filled bottle and floating it in waves about six to twelve inches high. the bottle will increasingly bob up and down, eventually submerge and sink. Longer or shorter waves will not affect it.

My American friends laughed at me when I recalled one low-level flight when I developed a sudden acute pain in my chest, suggestive of a coronary. On another occasion my passenger (his role was observer) responded to a much higher frequency, when his anal sphincter started to 'twitter', as he put it, accompanied by a craving to scratch his bottom, finally surrendering its integrity altogether, soiling his underpants. This episode led, unjustifiably, I felt, to cryptic comments about the quality of my flying 'scaring the ...' – you can finish it in whatever way you think appropriate!

Notwithstanding my stories, which were accepted in good humour, the Americans proceeded to set up experiments calculated to reproduce, in the laboratory, a vibrationary 'mix' similar to those likely to be experienced in a high-speed low-flying sortie. An aircraft seat was prepared for the metal platform which could be oscillated up and down by a powerful motor, and the 'buffeting' trials commenced, with some surprising results, though not altogether unexpected in the light of our Farnborough experiences.

As we were jolted vertically up and down through a carefully measured range of frequencies, so various parts of our bodies registered displeasure as the natural resonating frequencies were applied.

One man experienced severe chest pains – coinciding with the natural resonating frequency of his chest, which was confirmed as being seventeen cycles per second. He declined to continue the experiment as his father had died of a coronary not long before, and the pain which he experienced was too realistic. 'If God wants to call me, I want to be called in my bed, not on a shaking table.'

Another subject, on being vibrated at a somewhat higher frequency, had an unexpected but not entirely unwelcome bowel movement – he had been constipated for a week. He was encouraged by his colleagues to retire from the trials.

I lasted a little longer but, on a particularly 'rough' ride, the fillings in my teeth fell out, and I considered it prudent to desist before my teeth followed suit. The British Joint Services Mission, in Washington, were sceptical on receiving a dental account reading 'For replacement of dental fillings following an attack of "the shakes".'

All in all, we felt that we had overdone the laboratory simulation in that such extreme conditions were unlikely to be experienced in practice in the airborne situation.

To everybody's relief, the project was quietly terminated.

Before leaving the subject of 'vibration', let me mention that a similar problem had been experienced during the development of ejection seats by the British. In this instance it had not been the 'vibration' in itself but the rate of build-up of the acceleration force required to eject a pilot clear of his aircraft that had caused problems: if the build-up was too fast and too high and reached too high a level, injury would be sustained to the spinal column. For ease of storing survival equipment, survival rations were placed in the ejection seat between a pilot's seat and his parachute, upon which he sat during flight, and certain packs of survival food were found to 'absorb' the acceleration of the ejection force, causing a delayed but acceptable rate of build-up of force to the pilot during the ejection.

The moral of this tale is that, if any army marches on its

stomach, then perhaps it can be said that an air force ejects through its bottom.

Returning to the subject of acceleration, plans were in train to simulate acceleration effects likely to be encountered during the forthcoming maiden flight of the X-15 and – further ahead still – by astronauts when the technical problems of putting a man into space had been overcome.

We were joined in our experiments by men destined to become international heroes, as the American Space Program got under way – 'Scottie' Crossfield (the X-15 test pilot), 'Chuck' Yaeger (still smarting from watching the British film *Sound Barrier*, having himself been the first man to break through Mach 1 some time earlier) and Joe Walker (who went on to win the World Speed Record at Mach 3.31 – 2,196 mph). The same aircraft (X-15) also captured the World Altitude Record of 136,500 feet. I was privileged to participate in the centrifuge experiments simulating the X-15 flight envelope *and* to be able to operate the mock cockpit controls with realistic instrument response. (It is fully described in *The Right Stuff* by Tom Wolfe.) At the same time, I continued my efforts to get airborne as an alternative to being whirled around in the centrifuge like an egg in a mixer.

Suez was forgotten, and one day I was invited to fly a Cougar (F6F) by a man who had befriended me, Chief Petty Officer Pete Fowler, a competent pilot with combat experience in Korea.

The Cougar was a single-seat Navy jet, swept-wing fighter, designed to operate from carriers and, at that time, in front-line service. Though somewhat out of flying practice, I jumped at the chance. In accord with US Navy custom, Pete was to monitor my flight in another aircraft. He suggested that we climb to 25,000 feet and, when clear of all airways over up-state New York, indulge in a mock 'dog-fight'. I was to try to shake him off my tail. Being unfamiliar with the aircraft, I knew I was unlikely to succeed, but I did my best to pull tighter and tighter turns, both of us scribing the cloudless sky with vapour trials. It was exhilarating, even though Pete had little difficulty in keeping on my tail, and reminiscent of the days at Farnborough in the old Spitfire.

As I pulled more and more G, my vision dimmed, due to 'blacking out'. Suddenly, without so much as a 'here we go', the Cougar shuddered and went into a high-speed stall, flicked onto its back and started to rotate, fast. I looked up and saw a swirling blur of the New York State countryside, the vivid deep reds of the foliage mixed with the golden tints of the autumn coalescing into a kaleidoscope of colour. The aircraft rotated one way, then reversed into another turn, as I struggled to get it out of its inverted spin.

The altimeter was unwinding as though heralding a Wall Street crash, and this had the effect of concentrating my mind wonderfully. I heard Pete call on the radio: 'OK, Doc, you win. You can come out now.' Little did he know! By this time somewhat alarmed, I felt too pre-occupied to reply and continued to wrestle with the controls instinctively and from long-imbued training. I managed to recover at about 10,000 feet, having lost some 15,000 feet rather quickly, and we made our way back to Johnsville to land without more ado.

As we walked to the crew hut for debriefing, I was unsure what to say, fearing I might never be allowed to fly by myself again. To my relief, Pete broke the silence. 'That sure was some descent, Doctor, but I should have warned you that spinning is not recommended in that aeroplane.' His warm smile gave no hint of his inner thoughts. I could but agree with him, and could only reflect to myself that aeroplanes, like women, are quite unpredictable, though I felt I understood aeroplanes rather better.

14 *Beating a Retreat*

In 1958 I received a summons to return home, in the form of a letter bidding me, 'Call in, to discuss your future.' I felt like an eagle being captured to have its wings clipped. I felt a sense of helplessness. When I landed in Britain, it was to find a changed mood from that prevailing two years earlier, especially regarding the Services, which were continuing to run down – or being 'streamlined', as it was euphemistically put.

Reporting to the Naval Medical Department, I sought an opportunity to be rehabilitated into clinical medicine but was told that, owing to the shortage of medical officers, this would not be possible, and I found myself appointed medical officer in charge of the Naval Air Medical School at Lee-on-Solent. Here I found, not surprisingly, that little had changed. Successive generations of young naval doctors were still investigating the problems of urinating in an immersion suit without getting wet. One suggestion, that air crew should wear nappies, was not thought to be funny, and the offending medical officer was discharged. Erudite papers were continuing to be written on this and similar subjects, all of which were familiar.

Signs that I was getting old (at thirty-seven!) were beginning to appear: less agility on the tennis court; a propensity to black out when flying a tight turn. I was even beginning to read obituaries and was becoming intolerant, and people were beginning to address me as 'Sir'. The sparkle had gone. There were compensating benefits too, however. I was no longer frightened by women, and this was a most interesting discovery, requiring some serious self re-appraisal.

I recalled my father's advice, 'Never be the last to leave a party.' It was time to leave; this party, I felt, was on the wane, and so in 1959, with considerable reluctance, I submitted my request to the Admiralty to be transferred to the Retired List and set forth into an unknown and, initially at least, very inhospitable world, a world of very different standards, and yardsticks for measuring achievement, to the world I was leaving. I was ill-equipped, except for a determination to succeed. Notwithstanding this quality, the next ten years were traumatic, though not without education.

Through the following years, as a civilian, I continued to fly about in a light aircraft in a modest way. In due course I started to teach my son Chris to fly, as my father had taught me years before.

As time passed, I found caution becoming increasingly the watchword. I was mindful of the saying, 'There are old aviators, and bold aviators, but very rarely old, bold aviators.'

My eyesight was deteriorating. Not only had British Telecom thoughtlessly reduced the print size in their telephone directories, but – especially at night – the roadside billboards had become blurred. Poor printing standards, I concluded. The aircraft instruments were also less legible, so I didn't refer to them so much – after all, birds don't use instruments! Such is man's conceit and self-deception, especially with the 'wisdom' of advancing years. The day arrived when I was forced to wear spectacles to enable me to read the aircraft instruments at all.

One day (I had celebrated my fiftieth birthday by this time) I was showing a passenger how well a Beagle 'Pup' could perform aerobatics. The 'Pup' has a side-by-side seating arrangement and is fully aerobatic. In the thrill of getting airborne again, I forgot my age and pulled a considerable amount of G during some exciting manoeuvre. To my horror, the lenses in my spectacles fell out, into the bottom of the cockpit, there to be ground into powdered silicon, leaving my now useless frames on my nose, and as near useless eyes peering through them. Being above thick cloud at the time, I shamefacedly had to rely on my astonished passenger to interpret the instruments to enable us to grope our way back to the airfield.

Such is our inability to concede fallibility in ourselves. It was time to 'ground' myself – which I did immediately.

Epilogue: *Update, 1988*

Progress is not real and cannot be permanent
Henry George

Farnborough days were stimulating, exciting, adventurous, even in a way slightly dangerous, some might say, but, above all things that I learned, there was the fact that nothing is for ever.

By the very nature of the work one was always trying to keep ahead of the present. In the 1950s it would take about seven years between the time when an 'operational requirement' for an aeroplane was drawn up – in terms of speed, range, operating height etc – and the equipping of the first operational squadron. Once the operational requirement was sketched out by the Air Ministry, or Admiralty in some cases, aircraft companies would submit their own designs to what was then the Ministry of Supply. The next step was for the Ministry to place orders for one or two prototype aircraft, which would be evaluated by civilian and Service test pilots. In parallel with this, 'mock-ups' were made of the production aircraft design into which modifications could be incorporated, as experience was gained.

It was at this stage that medical and para-medical advice was called for before the detailed shape, size and environmental characteristics were irreversibly finalized.

To a certain degree the human body is adaptable to its

environment. Mentally, homo sapiens retains a great deal of versatility and ingenuity, but he is also fallible and limited by his bodily dimensions. The effectiveness of an otherwise ideal aeroplane can be considerably curtailed if a significant proportion of the pilot population has to be excluded on medical standards.

For example, Britain's Canberras could not be flown operationally by long-legged pilots, as they would have suffered knee injuries on ejecting. This could have been foretold by anthropologists.

The earlier Gloster Meteors and Hawker Sea Hawks were unpressurized. This required time-wasting screening of already experienced as well as all trainee pilots to assess their susceptibility to 'bends'. Not only was this time-consuming but the screening procedure itself was not wholly without risk by modern medical standards. In addition, it involved expensive modification of all unpressurized aircraft already in service.

Among examples of shortcomings in physiological equipment design, there was oxygen equipment, which required the pilot to turn his oxygen on when flying above 10,000 feet. All the written regulations in existence will not ensure a pilot's obeying them under stress, however slight. Such an omission cost the life of one Air Marshal when flying a Meteor solo in the Mediterranean.

I well recall the drama of watching from the deck of the salvage vessel as the wreckage of an Attacker aircraft was brought to the surface of the North Sea. As it broke surface, a fuel-selector lever could clearly be seen in the wrong position, and this had cost the pilot his life. There was no back-up warning system to remind the pilot why he was having increasing trouble in keeping his aircraft flying level, which eventually caused him to abandon it over the sea. His body was never found but the aircraft was located in sixty feet of water and the wreckage salvaged.

Design errors such as these, costly in terms of human lives, were gradually eliminated. 'Ergonomics' was a new word in the 1950s, and the Ergonomic Society had not long been formed. Surgeon Captain Geoffrey Fox Linton, my predecessor at Farnborough, was a founder member. Though not a qualified pilot, Geoffrey could hold any audience spellbound as a lecturer, and did much to further the cause of aviation medicine in the early days. His invaluable contribution to naval aviation was recognized by his being awarded an MBE.

But, for all this, a change could be discerned which was to alter the whole structure of British military aviation. For whatever reason, Britain was being outstripped by America with her vast resources in the development of airframe design.

Though Britain retained, at least for a considerable time, her technological ability in aircraft engine design, it was in the design of airframe and operations thereof that aviation medicine thrived. Development of new airframes by Britain was to shift to new concepts within the largely already explored flight envelope, rather than reach into new altitudes or speeds. An example of this is the successful Harrier. Within this trend aviation medicine was destined to change, with increasing emphasis on laboratory research rather than applied airborne research.

The TSR2, designed for fast low-level attack, with which I had been associated in the low-level flying experiments, was cancelled and Concorde was being advanced with abandon and without regard to commercial reality or cost. Politicians appeared unable to differentiate between technological excellence for military and commercial ends. Though a magnificent achievement technically, Concorde was surely doomed commercially before the first fare-paying passenger had checked in. At the same time Britain's defence policy was beginning to pursue a line of retrenchment (in spite of fine words by politicians to the contrary) which has continued to this day.

A lesson I learned from my halcyon days at Farnborough was the importance of avoiding entrenchment and to be prepared to adapt to a changing situation, even at great personal cost, rather than follow the conventional route being pursued by the herd.

On reading the proofs of this book, I was struck by the historical stamp of the story. It was almost carbon-dated, as if a very part of aviation history itself.

This impression was reinforced by seeing a Canberra aircraft in Ecuadorian livery in a little-used corner of Quito airport, clearly awaiting its destiny on the scrapheap. It was difficult to reconcile myself to the fact that what was once a prime unit in the defences of the United Kingdom was now considered outmoded by a Third World country.

I wondered if the progress of mankind had been paralleled in other fields of human endeavour. I decided to find out. A quarter of a century had passed since I had had contact with aviation, except as a fare-paying passenger, so I posed two questions:

Had the advance of technology enhanced the ability of man to operate aircraft more efficiently and safely?

Was there a correlation between the answer to the first question and other technologically advanced aspects of modern living?

I started my researches by revisiting my old haunts at Farnborough and was not altogether surprised to find it unrecognizable: a vast complex of new buildings; high security; administrative blocks; many more people, and of a different calibre. Where, I wondered, were the people who actually produced the results of research, and what was the nature of the research? I sensed a feeling of 'specialization' on a narrower part of the physiological spectrum – doubtless of a high academic calibre, but of a narrower application. Bigger filing cabinets (now termed 'data banks') and computers abounded everywhere (one room carried a notice 'Computer Consultant'). Not unsurprisingly, the aircraft (and doctors to fly them) had been largely replaced by 'medical scientists'. Research, once conducted in an airborne laboratory, was now conducted in a clinically controlled environment. It was most impressive, and yet I felt uneasy.

On enquiring as to details of research projects being conducted, I found that much of the hardware seemed familiar – though highly classified. It was as though the whole research effort had turned into a monolith, caught up in its own inertia, with diminished application in relation to the effort and cost involved.

I next turned my attention to what was happening in America, and visited an old American Air Force physician who used to fly with me when he was on exchange posting to Farnborough. He was now conducting some excellent research into Circadian Rhythm dysfunctioning ('jet lag') and had at his disposal a modern 727 simulator as well as a projected flight-deck simulator intended for use in the 1990s and into the next century. It was rewarding to find that, after twenty-five years, I was quickly able to 'fly' the simulator. With the projected instrument layout intended for the next generation of aircraft, I felt the cold shiver of a credibility gap. Not that the control layout was illogical or 'bad' *per se*: it was as though the human operator was being made redundant, but nobody had recognized this (or was brave enough to say it). The controls and switches no longer had to be *moved*; it was sufficient to touch them (or some cases just to speak to them – 'voice activated'). Why stop there? Perhaps a glance would suffice – even a thought, if the brain's alpha rhythms could be coded into the computer circuit. It seemed but a short step to the time when the old-fashioned pilot would be designated 'flight consultant'.

Disturbed by what I discerned as computer-dominated travel, I sought reassurance from the ageing flight-deck crew on a trans-Atlantic flight. They were only too pleased to talk – it relieved the boredom. In the space of fifteen months, I made some dozen trans-Atlantic crossings, and spent a lot of time talking to the flight-deck personnel. It was not reassuring.

Though perfectly competent in their role, and a more pleasant collection of men would be difficult to find, they all had one problem in common. Their flying lives were made up of brief periods of activity interspersed with long periods of boredom: boredom with ninety per cent of their eleven-hour flights, boredom with the repetitive nature of their task, boredom with combating the effects of jet lag, and lacking the exposure to the new, different challenges commonly found in most walks of life.

I discussed the problem with a number of aircrew and studied (and videoed) their behaviour during the active part of their flights (landing etc). One could discern a degree of excitement during these active periods, which one associates with a shipboard atmosphere on nearing a home port, and alertness was at a high level, as sophisticated skills were brought into play. During the long period of the transit part of the flight, boredom was manifest, associated with drowsiness (yawning etc). It is not surprising, therefore, that a special unit has been set up at Farnborough to log 'near-miss' incidents, involving human failures amongst aircrew. Sleep has featured frequently in these reports – that is, falling asleep whilst flying the aircraft. It has even been reported that there are official ways of warning flight-deck crew when they actually fall asleep. It would be more applicable (and safer) if interest and tasks (artificial if necessary) were to be built into the system to retain the (waking) attention of pilots during the boring periods.

I enquired of one captain when he last 'flew' an aeroplane. His reply was revealing. With the high degree of automation being introduced into flying and landing modern commercial aircraft, airline captains are now encouraged to fly light aircraft 'in order to keep them in flying practice.'

The time has come when, in order to curtail the power

of the computer, it might be wise to put 'stops' (like a synapse in neurological terms) in computer programs, beyond which a computer could not 'sense' without further authority from a human. Perhaps the current 'fail safe' philosophy could be replaced by a 'fail danger' philosophy.

A start has been made in the financial world, where restrictions have been placed on how much a share price can be allowed to move on the instructions of a computer, without 'authorization' by a human.

Before we abdicate too much responsibility to computers, we might reflect on the words of John Curran, in a speech he made in Dublin on 10 July 1790:

> The condition upon which God hath given liberty to man is eternal vigilance; which condition if he break, servitude is at once the consequence of his crime, and the punishment of his guilt.

In the context of this book, flying is certainly a field where we should pause before relegating the human being to 'the back burner'.

We will renege from our responsibilities at our peril.

Today, nearly half a century later, I look back to my navy days with reflective pleasure. They were days when adventure was a keynote, but with a serious purpose. They can never be repeated. I recall, with pride, the privilege of working alongside, and being accepted by the maritime aviators who were professional in the way they applied their flying skills, to the tasks confronting them.

I have nothing but the happiest memories of those men, many of whom still appear to regard me with some affection – to my never-ending surprise!

Appendix I

Types of aircraft flown by Dr W.H.B. Ellis

Tiger Moth
Harvard
Firefly Marks 1 and 5
Seafire Marks 15 and 17
Spitfire Mark 22
Barracuda 3
Dominie
Airspeed Oxford
Seafury
Anson
Meteor Marks 4 and 7
Vampire Mark 3
Martinet
Sea Otter (Flying Boat)
Mosquito T3 and 34
Lincoln Mark 2
Beaufighter T10
Sea Prince
Prentice
Cessna 150 and 175
Beagle Pup
Desford (prone position)
Attacker
Valetta
Devon
Balliol

Storch
Canberra B2
Sea Hornet
535 (prototype Swift)
DH110 (prototype Sea Vixen)
Avro 707 (scale model Vulcan)
Viking
Avenger
Sea Hawk Marks 1, 3 and 4
Hunter F1
Sea Venom 21
Javelin
F6F (Hellcat)
R4D (Dakota)
T28
F2H ('Banshee')
F9F (Cougar)
Chipmunk
(X-15/Simulator)
Prone Meteor

Aircraft-carriers landed aboard
HMS *Indomitable*
HMS *Vengeance*
HMS *Bulwark*
HMS *Illustrious*
HMS *Albion*
HMS *Ark Royal*
USS *Intrepid*

Appendix II

Obituary of GROUP CAPT H.P. RUFFELL SMITH (Published in *The Times*, 5 August 1980)

Group Captain H.P. Ruffell Smith, AFC, who died at his home at Thatcham on August 4, was unique amongst a small number of professional medical pilots. Born in 1911, educated at Highgate School, London, and Corpus Christi College, Cambridge, he qualified MB, BChir at the London Hospital and later gained his MRCS and LRCP.

The outbreak of the Second World War saw him already in the Royal Air Force, learning to fly. He was appointed to Flying Training Command as Flying Personnel Medical Officer, and later to Second Tactical Air Force, gaining experience in a wide variety of aircrafts in many operational situations, including the Berlin Airlift, flying many sorties studying fatigue in aircrew. After the war he developed and directed the Flight Section at the RAF Institute of Aviation Medicine, Farnborough. He initiated many in-flight human experiments in the varied operational aircraft at his disposal, always subjecting himself first, and few aircraft flying today do not carry some evidence of his research into instrument presention or cockpit layout. He won the respect of many friends at the then Ministry of Supply, Air Ministry Operations Division, and Admiralty Fleet Air Arm Test pilots of that era sought his advice on many and varied aspects of prototype aircraft evaluation.

He flew some 3,000 hours in approximately 80 different aircraft types, many of them prototypes. He is believed to be the oldest pilot to have done an initial decklanding on an aircraft carrier. Essentially a practical man, he landed a Mosquito on a frozen lake in Norway to simulate actual survival conditions to evaluate survival equipment. He held the AFC and two Bars, the only medical officer to gain three AFCs.

He belonged to many learned societies, but was particularly pleased to be a founder member of the Ergonomics Research Society; Chairman of Council, and Past President of the International Ergonomics Association.

After retiring from the Air Force in 1961, he turned his attention to safety at sea, and the design of driving cabs of heavy commercial vehicles – (typically) obtaining a heavy goods vehicle licence, but was persuaded to return to study flight safety in commercial airline operations, moving to California in 1975, where his services were in demand from a number of corporations as consultant, including British Airways, NASA, and various aircraft manufacturers. He was a member of the World Health Organisation Expert Advisory Panel on Occupational Medicine.

He held a pilot's licence till shortly before his death.

By nature modest, he appeared at times difficult to approach. Quick to deflate pomposity, and with a wry sense of humour, he was also a kind loyal friend. His courage was exemplary during his final long illness.

He leaves a widow, Annette, a son and daughter.

W.H.B.E.

Index